Urban Forest

Kolabs: Briefing

Kolabs—Kooperatives
Labor Studierender

In the context of *Wohnungsfrage*, Kolabs—Kooperatives Labor Studierender (Co-operative laboratory of students) acts as a client, commissioning an architectural design for a target audience of students and trainees. Central to our work is the development of a residential project that opens up new forms of communal living.

We understand ourselves as stakeholder-representatives for students and trainees—a social group that also includes us, as members of Kolabs. We all come from a university background and some of us have also completed company-based vocational training. Our constellation derives from young, politically active, and experimental practitioners, theorists, and analysts who each bring with them distinctive expertise: some of us are involved in artistic, architectural, and artisanal projects (Schlesische27, raumlaborberlin), while others are based in a university setting and provide new impulses from the fields of architecture, political science, education, and sociology. Additional impulses within our group originate in social commitment, e.g. Studis gegen hohe Mieten (Students against high rents) and ecoFavela Hamburg, and direct experience with alternative housing projects. However, what brings us all together is intensive and critical engagement with the themes of housing, participation, and architecture.

Together we have developed a brief for a new residential concept for people in the educational process that is to be formulated spatially and realized in a 1:1 model by the architectural firm Atelier Bow-Wow.

This housing concept is intended as a prototype beyond established forms of student housing such as student halls, shared, or single apartments. Its principal aim is to improve the quality of housing available to our target audience by strengthening possibilities for networking, exchange, and sharing.

Students and trainees often live in precarious financial conditions and in situations that are liable to constant change concerning their work, social, and academic environment or daily schedules, entailing frequent relocation and short-term life planning. Nevertheless—and against a growing shortage of affordable housing—the target group lays claim to homes in the inner city and thus participation in its social and cultural life. This fluctuating and multiperspectival way of life for many young people is central to our housing concept and our self-understanding. Kolabs supports the creation of a housing form that enables identification with the architecture and its appropriation, as well as the sharing of knowledge and resources.

Our concept depicts a new-build residential project that is conceived for long-term existence. It is intended to provide a basis upon which a utopian way of living can be developed for people in the educational process. We place great value on economic, environmental, and social sustainability.

A living environment that can be appropriated, and in which living, working, and togetherness is possible, is to be established for a collective community of thirty people. At center stage is an interface—a central space for collective use—that gives spatial expression to the alliance of these functions—and of the transition from public to communal to private realms.

Analogous to the reality of the lives of the people we represent, our group is a temporary collective for a project-related articulation of our housing vision. For us, these are prototypical and adaptable concepts open to further development by others—the evolution of Kolabs is inscribed in the conception of our group. What is important to us is not so much the constellation of the housing vision, but the ideas that we create, formulate, share, and carry on.

Target Audience and Group Size
for the Residential Project

In the following, preliminary reflections shall be made about the target audience and the size and composition of the group for the proposed household community. The target audience is, in general, made up of people in the educational process. This encompasses students and trainees, but also includes people who consider themselves to be open to learning, even though they are not seeking a formal educational degree from any institution. Curiosity and a desire to learn, an interest in building networks, and finding joy in imparting knowledge to others are what distinguishes the residents. Accordingly, it is our goal to create a place that promotes this exchange and a collaborative form of work, and which inspires the residents. For our target audience, the presence of networks is of great use for life in the city. The notion of networks also pertains to common living quarters and environments that establish social connections and yield organizational and financial relief. The collective community, where everyone shares their daily lives, should be an important point of contact—for orientation, to make friends, to look beyond the boundaries of one's own life-world, and to learn from others and support each other. Below, we conceive a model for a community of thirty people—a size that allows on the one hand both an environment in which to build trust and the ability to organize and reach agreements among the group and, on the other hand, offers the residents both a large network in which people with diverse perspectives and potentials can come together and in which each individual can reach their potential.

The desire is to create a project that offers the equal options of being alone, part of a small group, or together with all the residents. A project that offers people an opportunity for exchange and can bring many people, each with their own ideas and concepts, closer together while maintaining its comprehensibility. The infrastructure of the building—the kitchen and bathroom situation—must be organized in such a way that the daily routine runs smoothly. How this works will be clarified in the section "Utilitarian Spaces."

Economic, Ecological,
and Social Sustainability

Economic Sustainability

To begin with, and as a prerequisite for everything else, habitable space must be affordable. Our goal is to realize the project by financing it with a loan without requiring the residents to invest capital of their own in advance. The legal status of the building should transfer to a co-operative or association property. In so doing, we seek to enable the building to reside outside the speculative housing market and guarantee stable rents for the future. No one shall have sole control of the building or be in a position to profit from it. The rental income should be set in order to ensure that repayment of the loan, maintenance of the building, and support of the collective as well as other projects, can be financed sustainably. To reach this goal, solidarity models are also conceivable in which the residents pay more or less in accordance with their capacity and situation in life. We envision that the building is managed collectively and democratically by the residents, for instance by assigning posts on a rotating, temporary basis for limited terms of office. In exchange for this commitment, subsidized rent incentives are conceivable. As part of the ongoing process, we want to gather expert knowledge on this subject area and work out a detailed, realistic organizational model.

Environmental Sustainability

Environmentally sustainable architecture is important to us. The building should, as much as possible, be constructed from sustainable raw materials and exploit the full potential of renewable and green technologies, thereby reducing the ecological "footprint" and making a positive contribution to urban development. At the same time, we attach importance to long-life spans of the infrastructure.

Social Sustainability

Social sustainability, in terms of a viable structure of residents that can renew its members over the years, is also sought. This includes well-reflected treatment of issues of intergenerationality in the context of demographic change. The network idea pertains not only to working together, but also to social interaction. Sharing knowledge and providing mutual support are essential here. This notion is to be brought into the neighborhood, especially via the multifunctional realm described below, which links the project with the public sphere.

Building Type / Site

The decisive factor for selecting the site is access to social and spatial networks. In Berlin, the transition between an inner-city building plot and one on the periphery is often fluid. The immediate environs of the neighborhood, with its possibilities for shopping and nightlife, access to public transportation, and proximity to urban and near-natural open spaces, are aspects that constitute the quality of the site for young people in vocational training. Even if they have few financial resources and little political influence, people in the education and vocational training processes have the right to a site that enables them to participate in the social life of the city. Experience shows that our site criteria, coupled with the potential resident profiles described, would open the floodgates to the gentrification of a neighborhood. We must remain aware of this dilemma in order to counteract this process wherever possible. While we admittedly cannot solve the problem of gentrification, we do want to offer a deliberate signal for deceleration and critical examination of these processes. For instance, through a guarantee for rents that are stable and affordable for the target audience; intentional non-commercial use of the spaces; preventing the purchase of the project by individuals or investors; and by opening it up to the social inclusion of people who have limited financial resources.

Among many different sites and types of buildings, each offers unique potential compatible with our spatial concept: gaps between buildings, open spaces, roof-top areas, prototypical existing buildings such as factory spaces, supermarkets, car lots/garages, etc. We want to retain the possibility of applying the concept to a great many of these buildings and situations.

Many large cities as well as lively, culturally diverse smaller cities are characterized by increasing densification, a steady influx of people, and, as a result, rising rents. Prototypical old buildings are thus becoming scarce and unaffordable. In this context, finding a site for a multi-story building seems likelier to us. Hence we opt for a prototypical new building. The basic structure of the building can possibly be based on prototypical elements, to enable a relatively inexpensive type of construction that also allows its application to other locations. A parking lot/garage principle with split-levels would be conceivable, for example, but with floor-to-ceiling heights that are common to housing.

Spatial
Program

Our goal is architecture whose spatial characteristics not only foster being alone and being in groups of various sizes, from small to large, but also make these choices attractive. By introducing shared areas, we want to offer a diversity of spaces that allow for a multitude of functions despite the limited financial resources of the residents. Within the household community, there should be zones of varied nature: private, communal, and public. The—occasionally fluid—transition between these zones is the core element of our concept. This is where realms of the "in-between" emerge to fulfill different functions.

Spatial elements should be capable of being arranged variably in relation to each other. Furthermore, there should be a clear opportunity for the residents to plan, renovate, or expand independently. This should not be misconstrued as a demand for non-planning, but rather it expresses the desire for an architectural system that allows for unexpected creative living situations.

Interface / Communal Spaces

For us, the core of the project is the main interface—the central space for collective use. It primarily facilitates and encourages communication and exchange processes in the project. A transition takes place within the interface: from a large, bright, and sometimes loud core—where the entire household community can come together—to quieter, darker niches, which enable retreat, and establish a relationship to the private dwelling units. Within the interface there is a long table—around which all thirty residents can sit to eat, talk, and make new friends. This area is to have direct access to the kitchens.

Beyond that, the interface represents the negative areas resulting from the private rooms and utilitarian spaces, which means it also includes reinterpreted, enhanced circulation areas. All private and utilitarian spaces should be intertwined with one another such that the desired heterogeneous common rooms emerge from the logic of the interweaving. Reflecting different communication requirements, the interface area should be spatially heterogeneous and designed to be capable of appropriation.

For subdivision of the interface, methods of psychological space-planning should be employed so that the building's transitions from public to communal to private become evident. A spatial program such as this envisages no closed doors but physical and perceived thresholds—we are thinking here of platforms, lighting, and color design, semi-open room dividers, movable spatial elements, niches, visual axes, loges/balconies, lairs, split-levels, and so on.

The smaller leisure areas at the edges of the interface should have different atmospheric qualities: we envisage seating areas with smaller tables for activities such as board games, drinking coffee, eating food, or for relaxation and quiet activities. There should be a diversity of options for positioning and linking, which invite activation and exploration of the space. Visual connections and niches play a role in this regard.

Private Realm

Each resident should have the option of a lockable space of 15 sq m for private use. These private rooms should be bright and spacious so that their inhabitants feel comfortable and secure. It would be conceivable to make these rooms available in various types with different atmospheric traits and different degrees of fit-out. This includes the option of autonomously adding more private rooms. It would also be conceivable to have some areas in the building that are only equipped with the required infrastructure and utility connections, in order to allow self-build architecture. Despite the capability for individualized appropriation and possibly different formal characters of the private rooms, these should yield an ensemble. A repetitive hallway with anonymous, cell-like rooms is not an option for us.

Utilitarian Spaces (Kitchens / Bathrooms)
In the spatial fabric, the kitchens and bathrooms are the connecting links between the private rooms and the interface. Kitchens and bathrooms are shared by only small groups of people for the sake of better maintenance and easier housekeeping. We want to promote interaction between all the project's residents. This we intend will be achieved in a casual way, by dissolving the classic apartment-sharing arrangement. Thus we conceive of no fixed assignment of specific private rooms to specific kitchens and bathrooms.

Kitchens
We envisage four kitchens, each designed for seven or eight people. They should be equipped with standard kitchen equipment, that is, a hob/oven, exhaust hood, sink, refrigerator, space for food storage, and a sufficiently large work surface. The atmospheric qualities of the kitchens can be different. One possible differentiation could also be a division into a vegetarian kitchen, a kitchen for cooking meat, a kitchenette, and a kitchen that is open to the larger communal space.

When coming from the private rooms, it should be possible to access the kitchens without having to pass through the central interface area with the large communal table. The kitchens should be designed so as to provide a small, more private place to sit alone for someone feeling a need to withdraw. At the same time, the kitchens should affiliate with the interface in such a way as to enable all the residents to cook, eat, and celebrate together.

Bathrooms
Each bathroom design should be for use by up to five residents; and the bathrooms should be distributed evenly over the entire residential area.

Circulation Space
As already mentioned, the circulation should not be developed as a mono-functional access space, but intertwined with the entire spatial fabric (see "Interface"). It should also give the residents an opportunity to access their private quarters without contact with the large communal area. The multi-faceted circulation system can facilitate individual appropriation of the house by its residents and help prevent rigid structures and patterns of movement.

Of the communal areas, only at the building entries, which represent the threshold between the household community and the city, should there be a door that can be locked, to give the residents a feeling of security. On the ground floor of the building there should be barrier-free and wheel-chair-accessible approaches and facilities.

Multifunctional Realm / Workrooms
The house should offer a multifunctional realm for creative and collective work. This area is envisaged as a place for work, not leisure. We would hope that, here, the architecture would be able to provide a framework in which the residents can develop their ideas. It would be imaginable to have a core of infrastructure (electricity and water connections plus toilets), around which flexible elements structure the space and allow individual appropriation. Access to these areas should be barrier-free wherever possible. The collective will finance the special features of this area. Exactly what features and equipment are provided here will be decided by the collective and is not predetermined. The multifunctional area should have a high degree of spatial flexibility and allow for the possibility of easily subdividing it into differently sized work areas or separate project spaces. From a quiet workroom, a photo lab, or a café to a rehearsal room or a noisy work-shop, everything must be conceivable and, depending on the configuration, also be able to function next to each other. The areas should allow public

access to the collective zones, and hence they should be oriented toward the public realm. Analogous to the way the central interface works (from communal to private), this area also establishes a gradation of privacy to the multifunctional area—from public to communal. The multifunctional area also serves to represent the project, inviting the public to engage with it, and to participate in its workshops. We can for instance imagine a combination of café/exhibition/workshop areas. At the same time, the installation of an "intimate" portion should be made possible, in order to meet the most diverse conceivable needs (e.g. the sports space leading into the "courtyard").

Open Space / Outdoor Areas

Like the interface—as its outside counterpart, so to speak—we are hoping for open spaces that analogously open up a range of different qualities and situations. Here, too, we envisage a mix of public outdoor spaces (connected to the project spaces) and communal and shared–private outdoor spaces, which can be used in different ways: as a barbecue area for the entire community, as quiet corners for reading or talking, and as areas for growing plants in beds or playing sports. These outdoor spaces should likewise be exciting and differentiated, so that it stimulates the residents' power of imagination and encourages autonomous design.

Conclusion

Brief Summary

Housing concept for thirty people (reproducible and expandable in multiples of thirty-person groups). **Interface** (reinterpreted and open-circulation spaces as negative of the private and utilitarian spaces, continuum from communal to private, contains areas for congregation and work, heterogeneous areas of varied character due to constriction/expansion/light/dark, contains large room with a table for all thirty people). **Thirty private rooms** (15 sq m, lockable, distributed evenly throughout the structure). **Six bathrooms** (with dimensions and fit-out for five people, distributed evenly throughout the structure). **Four kitchens** (each with dimensions for seven or eight people, standard kitchen equipment, with seating area, close to the large communal table, and with direct access from the private rooms possible). **Multifunctional realm** (communication area accessible to the public, independently accessible from public and communal areas, adaptable and divisible form, barrier-free, gradation of public to communal analogous to the interface). **Open space/outdoor areas** (heterogeneous areas of varied character, continuum public–communal to shared–private).

Final Reflections

All told, in conceiving this project we have encountered a series of issues that need to be resolved, or architecturally interpreted, as part of the design.

First, there is the issue of the relation between public, collective, and private realms: How can the architecture promote the use of shared spaces and, at the same time, afford everyone the freedom of refuge and repose?

Second, the issue of the relation between architectural differentiation and free configurability: How can an architecture that meets modern standards offer its residents a living environment that is easy to appropriate and establishes differentiated opportunities to design, modify, and expand one's own environment?

Third, and in essence taking in the previous items, the issue of inclusion: The project is progressive; aimed at a committed group of mainly young people in the educational process, who are striving for new social solutions. It should not however put anyone off; it should be available to everyone, including people who have never before thought about such a form of living. We want to challenge society and, at the same time, to pick it up where it is.

Our objective is to provide a multifaceted opportunity for interested visitors to become part of this discourse and also to take part in the exhibition that accompanies the project.

top: Workshop, Haus der Kulturen der Welt, Berlin, May 2015
bottom: Excursion, Prinzessinnengarten, Berlin, May 2015

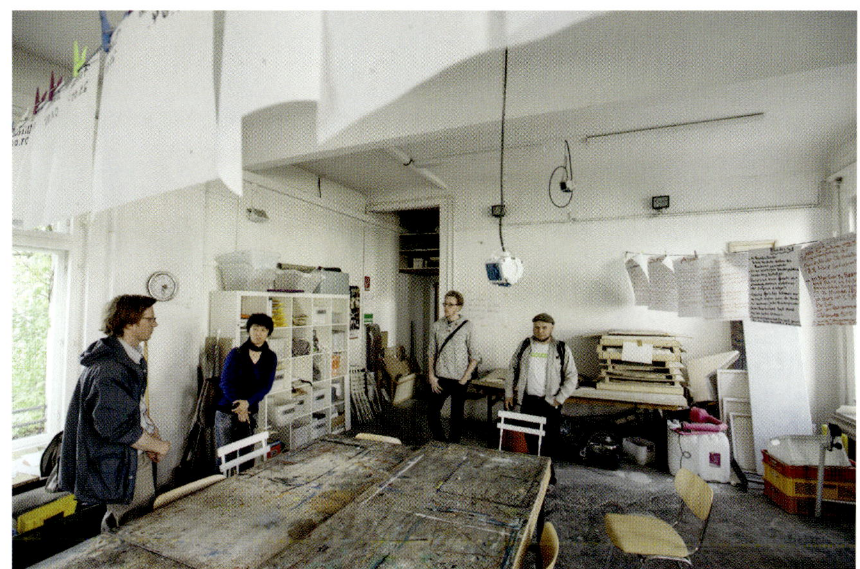

Excursion, Internationales JugendKunst- und
Kulturhaus Schlesische27, May 2015

Atelier Bow-Wow: Urban Forest

This is a 1:1 model of shared housing for young people, who, despite their wish to continue living in the city, find themselves priced out and virtually evicted by the speculative housing market. Sharing space and facilities is a strategy designed to compete against exclusive housing within the premise of private property ownership.

Sleeping capsules in various sizes, comprising units for individuals, are "thrown into the air" in order to leave the ground level open for an interface— a central space for collective use. A series of columns support the detached capsules at different levels. The fragmented, mezzanine floors inserted at the intermediate level, create clusters for communal use by connecting several capsules. The interstitial spaces between capsules are furnished with stairs, hanging closets, etc. The arrangement produces the double-height space at the center for collective use, including the workshop and the interface furnished with a table large enough to seat all residents. Bathroom and kitchen are installed among the columns.

A wooden post-and-beam structure has been applied to encourage hands-on participation during the construction process.

The direction—to "free the ground, live in the air"—was inspired by Italo Calvino's *Il Barone Rampante* (*The Baron in the Trees*, 1957) a story about a boy who escapes the "snail" dinners of his rich family and lives within the canopy of the trees for the rest of his life. In his arboreal surroundings, the boy is able to move from one tree to another without concern for land ownership. The boy's freedom is a critique of the social system at ground level dedicated to land ownership, and plays an important role in the revolution. His free spirit appropriates the forest and transforms it into an urban environment. "Urban Forest" is the place for today's "Barone Rampante" in a city like Berlin.

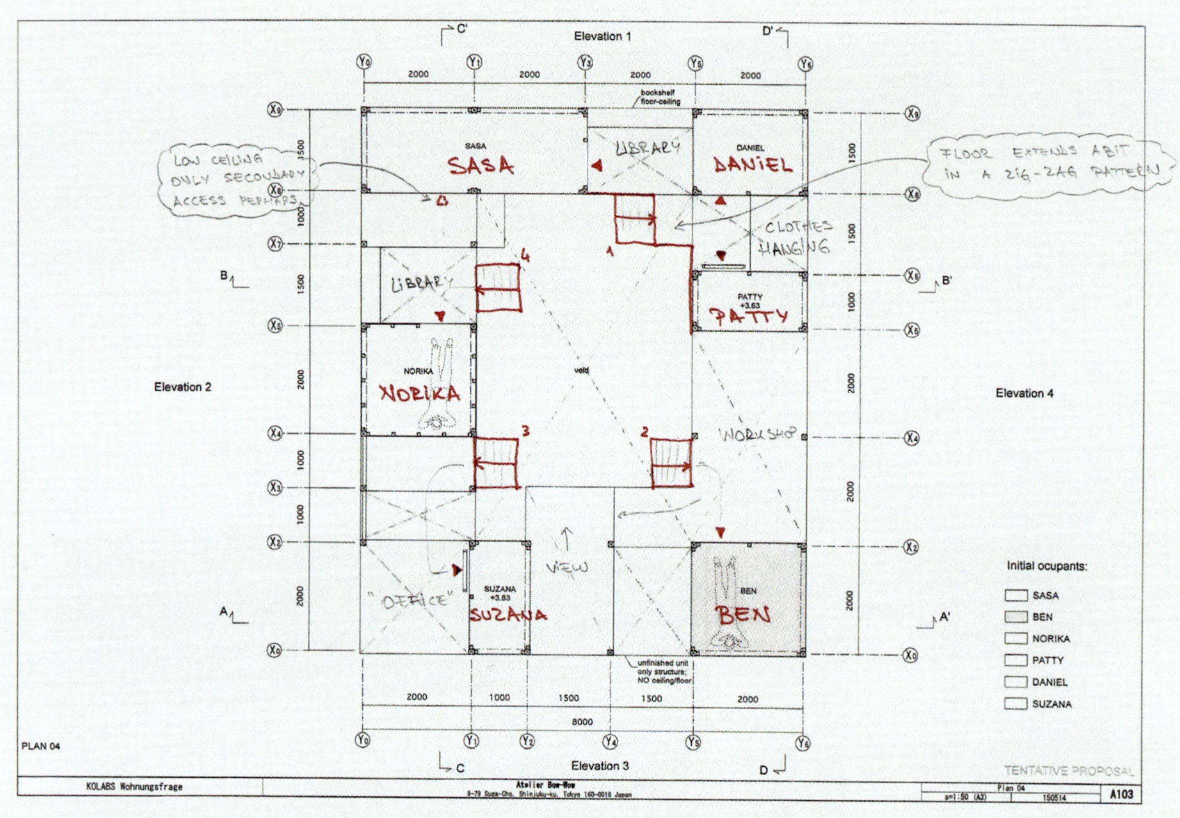
C'
Elevation 1
D'
Y0   2000   Y1   2000   Y3   2000   Y5   2000   Y6
X9
bookshelf
floor-ceiling
1500
1500
LOW CEILING
ONLY SECONDARY
ACCESS PERHAPS
SASA
SASA
LIBRARY
DANIEL
DANIEL
FLOOR EXTENDS A BIT
IN A ZIG-ZAG PATTERN
X8
X8
1000
CLOTHES
HANGING
X7
1500
B
LIBRARY
4
1
1500
X6
B'
1500
1000
PATTY
+3.63
PATTY
X5
X5
Elevation 2
2000
NORIKA
NORIKA
void
2000
Elevation 4
X4
WORKSHOP
X4
1000
3
2
2000
X3
1000
X2
VIEW
X2
2000
Initial ocupants:
"OFFICE"
SUZANA
+3.63
SUZANA
BEN
BEN
2000
A
A'
SASA
X0
X0
BEN
unfinished unit
only structure;
NO ceiling/floor
NORIKA
2000   1000   1500   1500   2000
PATTY
8000
DANIEL
Y0   Y1   Y2   Y4   Y5   Y6
SUZANA
C
Elevation 3
D
PLAN 04
TENTATIVE PROPOSAL
KOLABS Wohnungsfrage
Atelier Bow-Wow
8-79 Suga-Cho, Shinjuku-ku, Tokyo 160-0018 Japan
Plan 04
s=1:50 (A2)
150514
A103

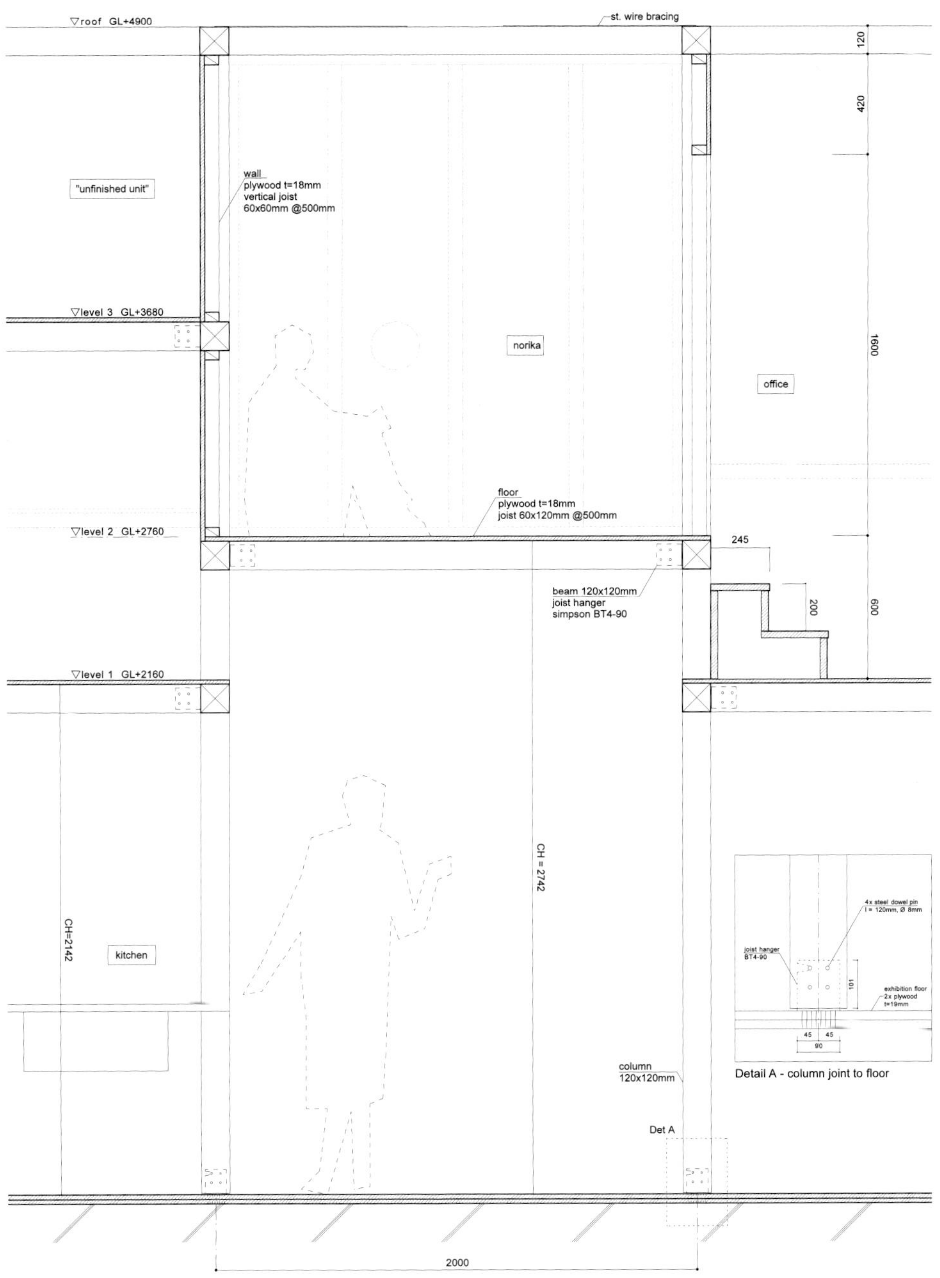

▽ roof GL+4900
st. wire bracing
120
420
"unfinished unit"
wall
plywood t=18mm
vertical joist
60x60mm @500mm
▽ level 3 GL+3680
norika
office
1600
floor
plywood t=18mm
joist 60x120mm @500mm
▽ level 2 GL+2760
245
beam 120x120mm
joist hanger
simpson BT4-90
200
600
▽ level 1 GL+2160
CH = 2742
CH=2142
kitchen
4x steel dowel pin
l = 120mm, Ø 8mm
joist hanger
BT4-90
101
exhibition floor
2x plywood
t=19mm
45   45
90
column
120x120mm
Det A
Detail A - column joint to floor
2000

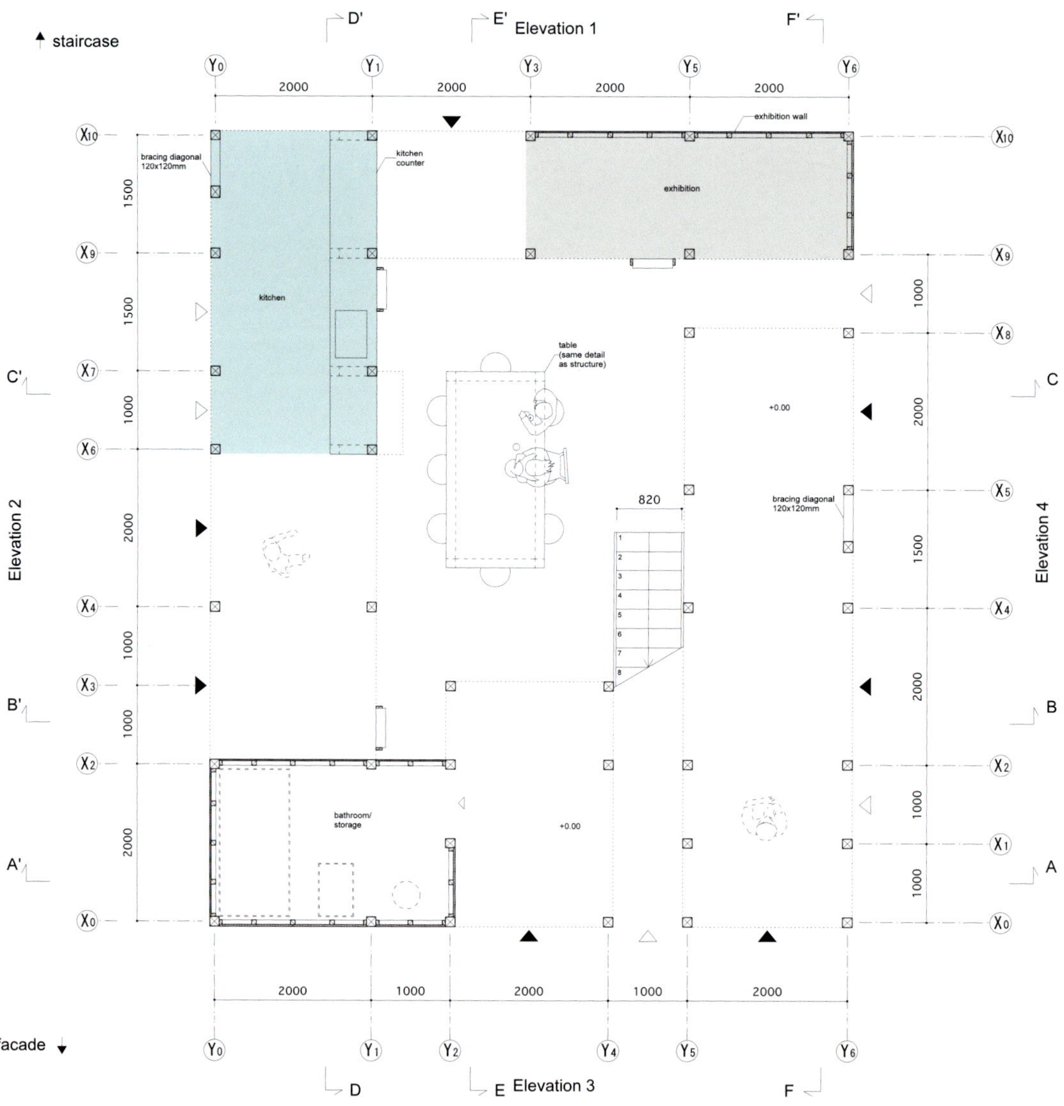

staircase
D'
E' Elevation 1
F'
Y0
Y1
Y3
Y5
Y6
2000
2000
2000
2000
X10
bracing diagonal
120x120mm
kitchen
counter
exhibition wall
X10
1500
exhibition
kitchen
X9
X9
1500
1000
table
(same detail
as structure)
X8
C'
X7
C
1000
+0.00
X6
820
X5
Elevation 2
2000
bracing diagonal
120x120mm
Elevation 4
1
2
3
4
5
6
7
8
1500
X4
1000
X4
X3
2000
B'
B
1000
X2
X2
bathroom/
storage
1000
+0.00
X1
2000
A'
A
1000
X0
X0
facade
Y0
Y1
Y2
Y4
Y5
Y6
2000
1000
2000
1000
2000
D
E Elevation 3
F

Plan GL+3200
s=1:50

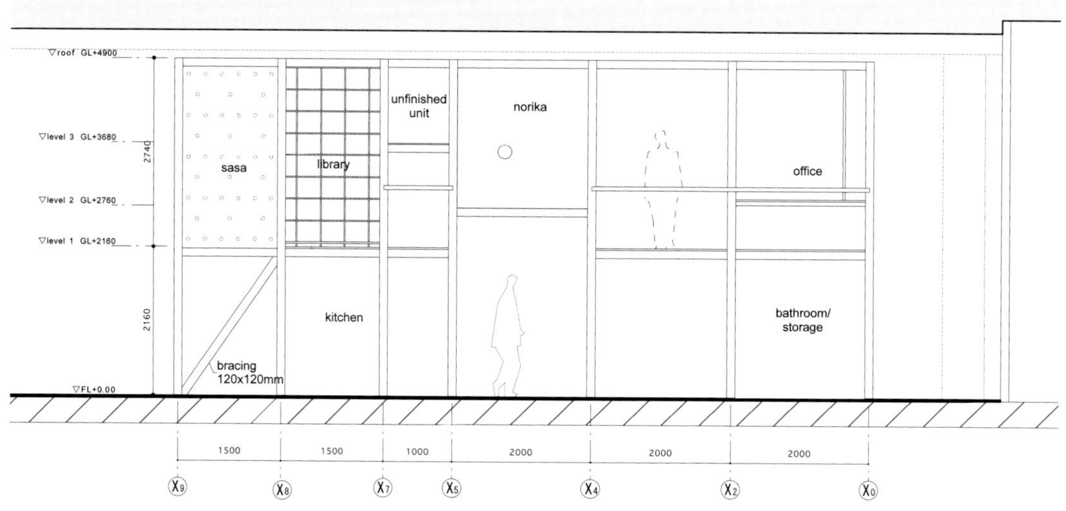

▽roof GL+4900
▽level 3 GL+3680
▽level 2 GL+2760
▽level 1 GL+2160
▽FL+0.00
2740
2160
sasa
library
unfinished unit
norika
office
kitchen
bathroom/ storage
bracing 120x120mm
1500
1500
1000
2000
2000
2000
X9
X8
X7
X5
X4
X2
X0

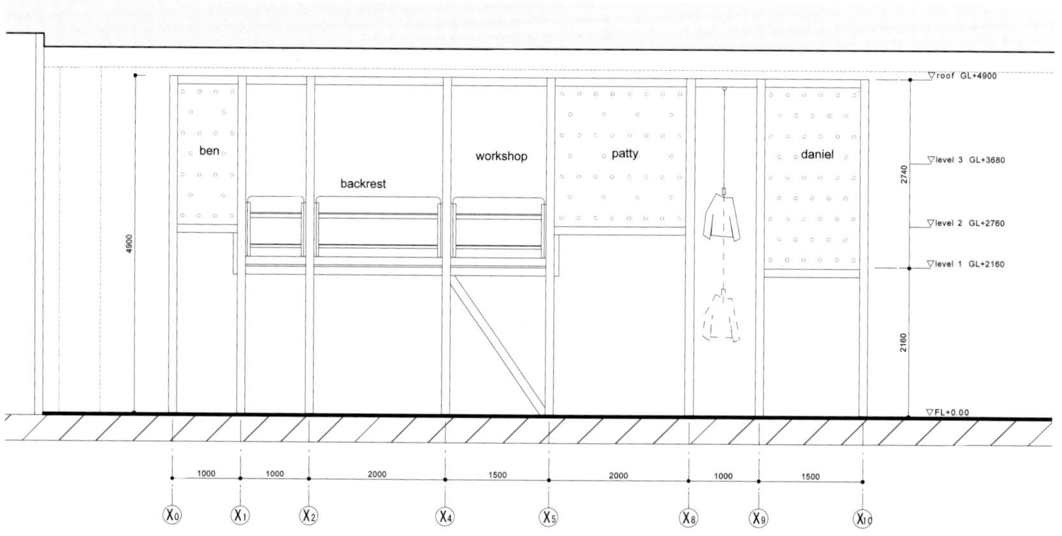

▽roof GL+4900
▽level 3 GL+3680
▽level 2 GL+2760
▽level 1 GL+2160
▽FL+0.00
2740
2160
4900
ben
backrest
workshop
patty
daniel
1000
1000
2000
1500
2000
1000
1500
X0
X1
X2
X4
X5
X8
X9
X10

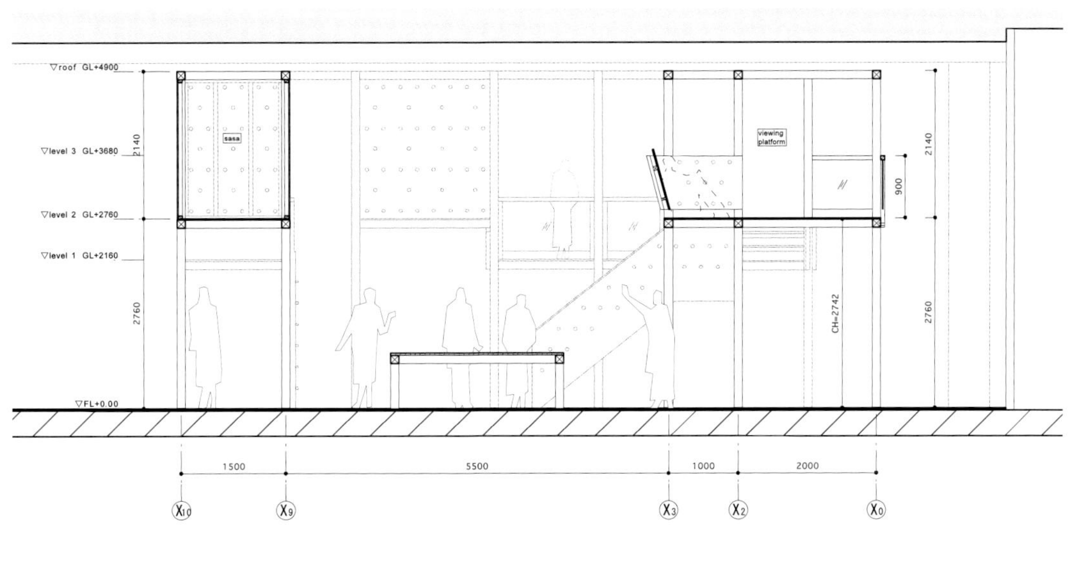

▽roof GL+4900
▽level 3 GL+3680
▽level 2 GL+2760
▽level 1 GL+2160
▽FL+0.00
2140
2760
sasa
viewing platform
900
2140
2760
CH=2742
1500
5500
1000
2000
X10
X9
X3
X2
X0

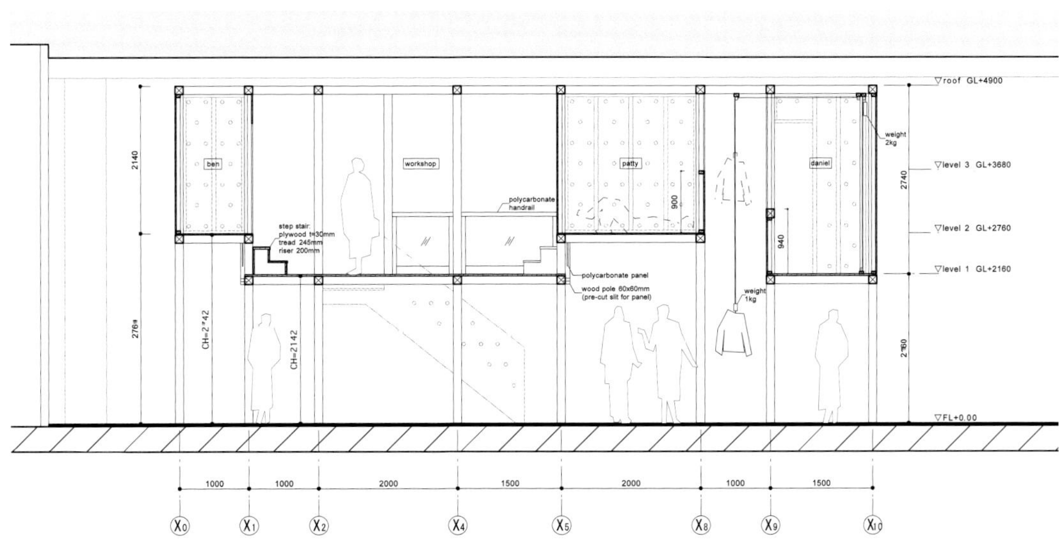

▽roof GL+4900
▽level 3 GL+3680
▽level 2 GL+2760
▽level 1 GL+2160
▽FL+0.00
2140
2760
CH=2742
CH=2142
beh
workshop
patty
daniel
step stair:
plywood t=30mm
tread 245mm
riser 200mm
polycarbonate handrail
polycarbonate panel
wood pole 60x60mm
(pre-cut slit for panel)
weight 2kg
weight 1kg
900
940
2740
2760
1000
1000
2000
1500
2000
1000
1500
X0
X1
X2
X4
X5
X8
X9
X10

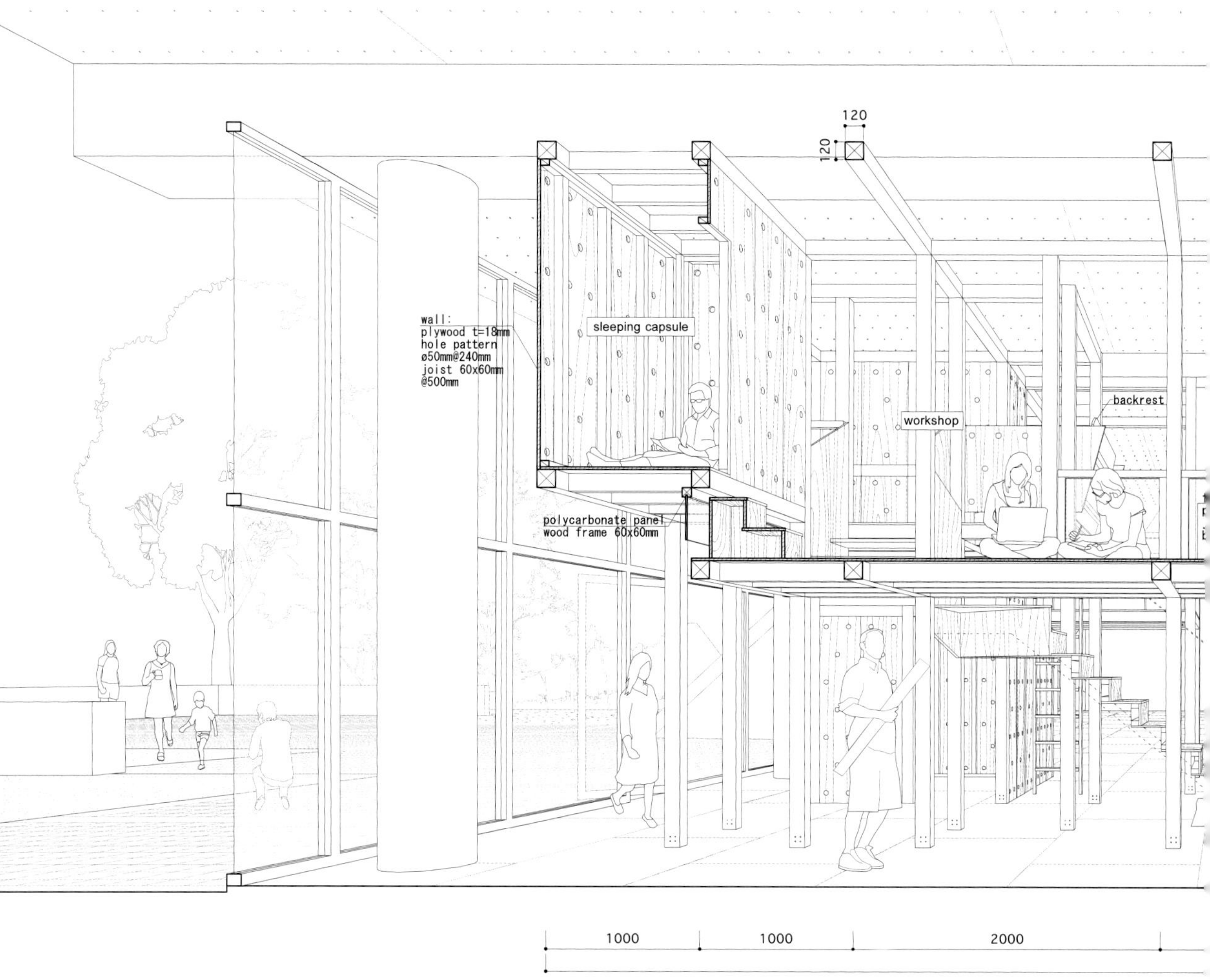
120
120
wall:
plywood t=18mm
hole pattern
ø50mm@240mm
joist 60x60mm
@500mm
sleeping capsule
workshop
backrest
polycarbonate panel
wood frame 60x60mm
1000
1000
2000

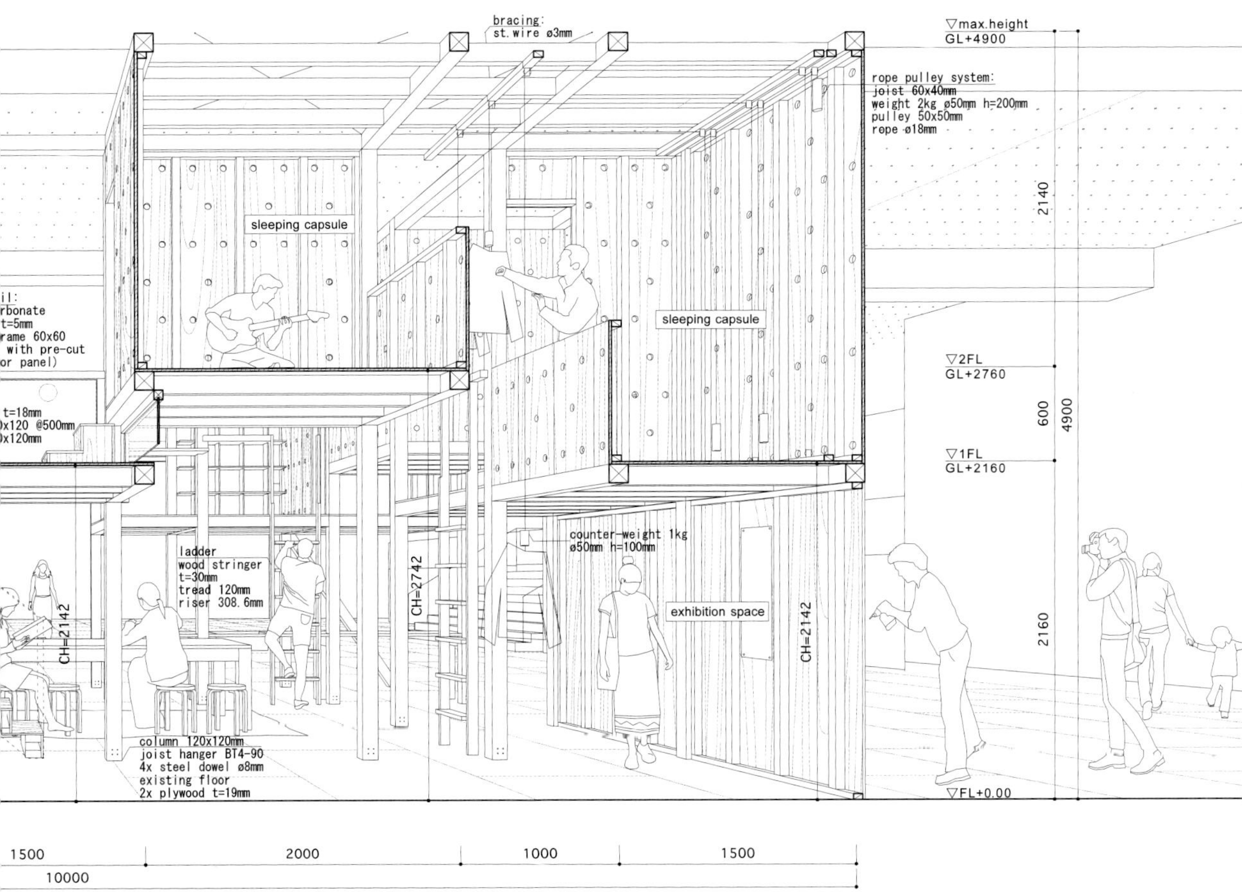
bracing:
st. wire ø3mm
rope pulley system:
joist 60x40mm
weight 2kg ø50mm h=200mm
pulley 50x50mm
rope ø18mm
▽max.height
GL+4900
2140
sleeping capsule
sleeping capsule
il:
rbonate
t=5mm
rame 60x60
with pre-cut
or panel)
t=18mm
0x120 @500mm
0x120mm
▽2FL
GL+2760
600
4900
▽1FL
GL+2160
counter-weight 1kg
ø50mm h=100mm
ladder
wood stringer
t=30mm
tread 120mm
riser 308.6mm
CH=2742
CH=2142
exhibition space
CH=2142
2160
column 120x120mm
joist hanger BT4-90
4x steel dowel ø8mm
existing floor
2x plywood t=19mm
▽FL+0.00
1500
2000
1000
1500
10000

Urban Forest, 1:1 model
Haus der Kulturen der Welt

Urban Forest, 1:1 model
Haus der Kulturen der Welt

Commonalities

Commonalities of Architecture

Recently one often hears expressions to the effect that we are rich but we don't know if we're happy. This seems to express an unease about a society and an environment that have changed since modernization, and a dissatisfaction about how things have become as they are, on the part of someone who doesn't know where they are. Since architecture has been a driver of modernization, it must surely bear a great deal of responsibility for this.

It is undeniable that the construction industry has worked closely with the restoration of cities after wartime devastation and the balanced development of Japan. In the name of protecting people's property and life, provision of social infrastructure by the "government," whether national or local, has progressed as never before. Rivers and roads have been treated as things where flows—of water and traffic—can be measured and structures of steel and concrete have been constructed to control these. As a result, rivers no longer flood but have been made unapproachable and roads have been simplified to be solely for traffic. A policy of encouraging individuals to own a house with land has also been adopted. Further, an engagement with making houses resistant to fire and earthquakes has motivated individuals to demolish old houses that do not meet these standards. Since new-house building means the purchase of the domestic electric devices and appliances, furniture, culinary equipment, beds, and other fixtures, the economic effects extend over a wide range of society. Thus, the industrialization of environmental conservation and industrialization of house building have resulted in a vast production of safe and convenient towns and homes. During this process, management by ordinary people, including care for mountains and villages to ensure a good environment, and houses being built from local materials by local builders, which were parts of the culture of daily life, have been shifted into the domain of industry. Commercial premises, which have occupied a greatly increased proportion of urban space as economic growth has progressed, have become evermore gigantic, with the aim of mobilizing customers, and created spaces that absolutely anybody can use, almost like public spaces. In exchange for money, people can make use of a clean and dependable space, where they are treated as customers and obtain a sense of satisfaction as "individuals." In this process, the urban behaviors such as relaxation and recreation, which formerly the people organized themselves, have been transferred into the so-called "service" industry.

Thus, there has been industrialization over a range of different areas, spurred by the miraculous growth in Japan's GDP during the second half of the twentieth century. But there have been some unexpected by-products of this process: people who do not know what kind of relationship to have with nature where they live, what kind of house should be built in their town, and how they can utilize public space for themselves. Not to know these is to be incapable of solidarity. And, if this is so, they are dispersed into "individuals," dependent on systems sanctioned by the "public/ government" and the market. Scope and opportunities to make their own decisions and behave autonomously have been gradually lost. And for people not to know this tends to help efforts to increase industrial productivity. This is because it is through the provision of the maximum number of choices, in terms of science, engineering, economics, and design, that the existence of the "individual" is confirmed. The result of sixty years of this kind of environment-making, house-making, and town-making is the appearance of the standard Japanese town. One could say that the fragmented and irregular impression it makes is interesting, but it cannot be interpreted, however hard one tries, as more than an aggregation of individuals. Sadly, individuals cannot rise above being individuals; and such individuals are lacking. What is lacking from this scene are typologies of architecture and people's behaviors that transcend generational differences, transcend subjects, and are commonly owned at their locus. In order to enable these local typologies and behaviors, not only must we become great "individuals," who design excellent architecture, but we must also become outstanding "people" transcending our generational and individual differences. Self-confidence and pride abound when it is possible to feel oneself a part of a group of outstanding people. Undoubtedly, it is because this feeling does not exist that we "don't know whether we are happy." In short, the weaknesses of contemporary industrialized architecture and urban spaces are most evident in scenes where commonality is most essential. Of course, there have been great losses due to earthquakes and warfare. However, there are also repeated dislocations and weaknesses associated with the organization of successor societies. Such organizations have a tendency to separate and refine the collectivity of people into pure "individual bodies" and pure "public bodies." One part of this tendency—the adventure in architectural practice, particularly in the latter part of the twentieth century that placed importance on the exalted individual—has, in our estimation, now reached its limits. If the twentieth century—which placed excessive emphasis on "individual" and "public"—has lost sight of the "common," let us now start out on the adventure of an architectural practice that shifts importance onto the "common." In this book, it is our intention to use the term "architectural commonality" to denote this area of the "common."

Commonality is an unfamiliar term, which only rarely has been used in the field of architecture. In fact, as far as we have been able to find, only the American architect Louis Kahn has previously used it. According to him, we are able to appreciate ancient buildings because something ageless, transcending place, communicates between human beings, and this is commonality. A similar sensibility is that expressed both by Jørn Utzon's

"innermost being of architecture," which holds that the present and past are linked by an anthropological intelligence inherent in architecture, and Christopher Alexander's "timeless way of building." These indications, that we who live in the present can have a communication with our consciousness and are the creators of those great buildings that seem to have arisen spontaneously from the earth, are inspiring. We would like the argument of this book to carry on this spirit. However, Louis Kahn's commonality, where buildings are experienced and appreciated, is used in a somewhat passive context. By comparison, the intention of this book is to apply commonality to architecture in a more active design context, beginning with the experience of buildings and urban space. For this, a medium capable of detecting commonality is necessary. We shall start from considering the states in which commonality is materialized, the circumstances in which it is manifest in a material context.

What we first envision is a situation whereby buildings, which are largely similar but have slight individual differences, occur repeatedly in a region or in a situation where they are arrayed in the same street. Although each of these buildings is the property of a different owner, it participates in the village or urban space through its roof and façade, and these elements transcend ownership to form part of the whole. This is evident through observations of multiple buildings. The common characteristics that transcend individual differences are termed the typology of architecture. However, typological understanding is for researchers, whereas commonality is when the people who inhabit the space have common ownership of the type of building. Typology of this kind is established when there are people that know what type of building is suitable for an area or town. Such people have pride in their own town and are full of self-confidence.

Another thing we envision is a situation in which people behave with freedom in a square or similar open space. Although, of course, it is rare for all behaviors to be completely discrete, we must focus on only a few behaviors. Here, a behavior is a form connected to a certain place whose repetition transcends differences in subjects. Due to this, it is possible for a place and time to be jointly owned by people who do not know each other, who are aware of their mutual differences, and who do not interfere with each other. Interestingly, a behavior that is repeated several times becomes a skill of the people performing it. Thus, a behavior belongs to each of the people and belongs to the place; it can be learned and cannot be monopolized by any one single person. Conversely, it is not easy to prevent another person performing the same behavior. A behavior is property belonging to the person who has learned it and, simultaneously, a commonly owned property. The behaviors of people who know how to behave have aspects that are sophisticated, gentle, and reassuring. And this is precisely why they are allowed to monopolize a shared space, albeit temporarily. This is the freedom allowed simply for being alive. And it is because of this that it is possible to be generous to others.

The common points between architectural typology and people's behaviors are that they are repetitive and transcend differences in subjects and individuals in a certain region or town. What makes this possible is type. Viewed over a long period, a type changes gradually while maintaining its characteristics as a type in some form or other. Type is associated with shape, but it is not autonomously and purely established as a pattern. A type is established when various factors, including climate, materials, way of life, social systems, and economics, are combined and achieve equilibrium. Therefore, by looking at types, we can understand that, in a world where infinite relationships are possible, there are some fixed mutual relationships between specific things.

The changes that types undergo over time are due to some of the many factors involved in this mutual relationship changing quantitatively, or becoming lost or other things combining with them, so that new equilibriums are found. For example, the balance with nature maintained by the works of a craft potter is different from the balance with nature of mass-produced ceramics. Whereas, for the former, the value of the work is in the fact that the shape is heuristically created through a dialogue with nature (the clay), the latter mobilizes large quantities of clay, individual differences are restrained, and the value is in products with no deviations. From a concrete and individual relationship with nature to the mobilization of nature for the purposes of mass production. Amidst the mutual linkages associated with ceramics, the interaction with natural elements regresses into an imperceptible background and what is known as localism is also lost. Genealogy is the re-understanding of these shifting mutual linkages as plastic, by the introduction of the measure of time to observations of these typological changes. Both the typology of architecture and people's behavior are produced repetitively amidst these mutual linkages. It is in such a sense that they show the conditions under which people live in a certain place.

The understanding of commonality from the typology of architecture and people's behavior is a development from behaviorology. In behaviorology, the behavior of natural elements, human behavior, and architectural behavior (repetitive typology) are addressed as behaviors that are repeated at their own rhythm, transcending differences in subjects. And we have observed the emergence of an architectural intelligence when architecture integrates these differing behaviors. Our argument was for the practical consideration of discrete problems using the findings obtained from observations of behaviors. For the observation of behaviors, we required a clear distinction between those behavior-producing factors that can be changed and those that are immutable. For example, the behavior of water flowing downward under the influence of gravity cannot be changed but the mode of the flow can be changed by the shape of the surface that carries it. In the case of street soccer, the physical skill of controlling the ball without using hands cannot be changed (or the game would not be soccer) but the size of the pitch and the goals can be changed and local rules used. These observations reveal that there are fixed patterns in the way things are connected; these are the mutual linkages between things. The concept of commonality is offered in order to produce a common resource, accessible to all, that makes it possible for these interlinkages to be perceived.

We consider that the logic of commonality, starting with typology and behavior and moving on to the mutual linkages, is of great importance. This is because the logic of commonality resists the progressive fragmentation of daily life today, particularly in urban areas. However, this resistance is not the previous schema that individuals have existed from the start and that resistance should rescue individuals oppressed by state and social systems. Rather, it is resistance to the idea that individuals have existed *ab origine*. This is because the original state of individuality is produced by its interdependence with the state and social systems. These are like the two sides of a coin. And one thing that is dismissed as if negligible in this process is the intermediate area of the "common." It is here that there should be an abundant commonality, learned by the individual and also belonging to the place. Viewed in terms of behavior, the individual is interpenetrated with the common and it is not possible to draw a rigid boundary between them. When dealt with within a public system, however, the problem is that this is treated as having too great variety. When this is so, it creates the hypothesis *ab origine* individuality and equality = the "empty body."

Twentieth-century architecture has played an important role in reinforcing this kind of illusion.

For example, modern apartment blocks and estates of detached houses are typical of this. Since, in particular, the apartment block—a form that played an established role in dealing with the postwar housing shortage—has a large supply of housing as a prerequisite, family units are overlaid onto housing units and uniform spaces are created by the repetition of this kind of equality. Amidst this equality, the totality of this communal housing is separated into the different areas of households (individual), areas that the residents of the apartment block jointly use (communal), and areas into which people from outside may enter (public). This separation into individual, communal, and public is replicated in floor area, which is measurable. As long as it is understood through this schema, the residents, whatever skills they may own, are assumed to be "empty bodies" without skills. Nevertheless, provided this is an apartment block, where an effort is made to find the "significance of living communally," the communal is devised as an area connected with the individual. However, once the domain of the communal is equated with surface area, as in this schema, it can only represent a concept of the communal. Since nobody knows how this should be used, all the rules concern the avoidance of trouble to others (no ball games, no noise, no fires), and it finally declines into a misapplied equality and, the costs of management notwithstanding, cannot be used for anything.

The empty-looking areas that are accessible to all, such as the open spaces created in front of public facilities, and the open areas created at the foot of multi-story buildings as part of the terms and conditions for relaxation of the floor-area ratio, require us to be "empty bodies." There is of course a requirement for a very large area of empty land around a multi-story building for the efficient evacuation of the public during an emergency. The size of this must inevitably correspond to the quantifiable total of individuals (or the total of quantifiable individuals). However, concentrating solely on this aspect and putting aside any consideration of its continuity with the urban space at ground level and its possible uses as part of the town, means that this will remain as flat, boring, open space.

With these assumptions of a useless "public" and a homogeneous "individual," the boundaries of the individual alone are regarded as inevitable. When such large-scale apartment blocks and open spaces are constructed according to this schema, people are disciplined into an understanding of the relationship between the individual, which accords to the schema that the total of quantifiable individuals is the totality.

The first challenge of architectural design where emphasis is placed on commonality is to challenge this "empty body" and the primacy of the individual symbolized by this. This challenge is particularly effective for housing where repetition is a condition, towns created by such repetition, open spaces where everyone may gather, and other areas connected to daily life. This no doubt reflects an awareness of issues such as the fragmentation of modern life, the obscurity of mutual linkages, and the transfer of matters that were once a part of daily life into the industrial domain.

Atelier Bow-Wow's design, which places emphasis on commonality, has developed in the following four areas:

First is the genealogy of housing. By introducing a time axis into housing typology and observing changes over time, it is possible to highlight those aspects of the mutual linkages that change and those that do not change. We have conducted research examining the history of a specific town through the transformation of the house-types, as in *Walking with Atelier Bow-Wow Kanazawa Machiya Metabolism* (2007)[1] and created new generations of existing typologies in individual housing design, as in *Split Machiya* (2010) and *Tower Machiya* (2010). In the background to this research and design practice, there has been a sense of semi-despair about Japanese architectural practice in the second half of the twentieth century. There are questions about why our generation cannot build excellent streetscapes and why we cannot produce vernacular architecture. Accordingly, even when creating individual houses, we design these as an answer to these doubts. What makes this possible is the genealogy of housing typologies, and it is our plan to produce a book giving more details of this when circumstances allow.

Secondly, there is the behaviorology of windows. Windows are where the most varied behaviors are concentrated in a building and windows are repeated in a region or town, transcending the individualities of the buildings. We have collected, measured, and compared these in cities throughout the world, examined the concept of windows, and located windows within society. First, in *Windowscape: A Genealogy of Windows*, we derived a concept of the window as a balance between a concern with sunlight, humidity, and other climatic and natural features, and a concern with religious norms and lifestyles. In *Windows 2: A Genealogy of Windows and Streets*, we discovered the repetitive behaviors of windows facing the street in a number of countries, and interpreted the formation of these behaviors in terms of a balance between the genealogy of the windows, the system of production, and the social system of which the windows are part. This was undertaken as a joint research project of Yoshiharu Tsukamoto's Laboratory at Tokyo Institute of Technology and YKK's Windows Research Institute.

Third are micro-public spaces.[2] These are works in which interventions are made in public space by the fabrication of small buildings, mobile structures, and large items of furniture within the framework of an art exhibition. The making of these works begins with a visit to the city and observation of the behaviors of people that characterize that city. We then consider what is produced by the repetitive behaviors, what skills are used, and how this is related to different kinds of environments and cultures. There are always spaces and tools that support such behaviors and these are transformed to suit all the possible scenarios. This is a social experiment, in which tales of the mutual linkages that form the place are in the foreground through the production of fictional behaviors and dispositions of people, which is a little different from normal. It is an act of resistance against the "empty bodies" assumed for the plazas created in the twentieth century. The Atelier Bow-Wow Micro Public Space exhibition, held from February 2014 at the Hiroshima Museum of Contemporary Art, shows a collection of such acts.

Fourth is the design of plazas and parks. The findings made in the Micro Public Space experiment were put to use in the design of permanent public spaces within the actual urban space. By conducting workshops and interviews from the earliest stages of the design, we discovered several of the potential users of the public space and modified the environment in a direction in which their behaviors could be spontaneous and form a synergy with the other users of the space. By involving people in a discussion about the management of the new square, we attempted to create an opportunity for contact between the citizens and government authorities and develop this as far as community planning.

1   See Atelier Bow-Wow, *Walking with Atelier Bow-Wow Kanazawa Machiya Metabolism*, exhibition catalogue (Kanazawa: 21st Century Museum of Contemporary Art, 2007).

2   See Atelier Bow-Wow, *Micro Public Space*, exhibition catalogue (Hiroshima: Hiroshima Museum of Contemporary Art, 2014).

Methodology of Behavior and Relationships: A Conversation with Koki Tanaka

Yoshiharu Tsukamoto:
I had an opportunity to see your video installation *abstract speaking—sharing uncertainty and collective acts*,[1] and I was pleased to notice a part that was in common with what we had been thinking: an awareness of the earthquake and tsunami in Japan of March 2011, even though this was not expressed overtly.

Your video shows a single act performed by multiple people. In order to consider quite what this is, we will locate the relationship between people's behavior and the creation of things and sites within a matrix of "people and skills." For example, painting and sculpture—the act of creativity using one's own skill—can be described as creation by an individual as an integrating subject. The matrix it fits into is *person (singular) : skill (singular)*. In the case of architecture, buildings cannot be created if there are no skilled practitioners, hence *persons (plural) : skills (plural)*. An orchestra is similar. In the park of the Temple of Heaven in Beijing, people gather in the early morning between the trees, grown in grid form, to carry out their preferred exercises. These include tai chi, ballroom dancing, battledore and shuttlecock—hitting a shuttlecock to keep it in the air, walking backwards up and down a slope, and massaging ones back against the knots of the trunk of an ancient tree. Here a single group is *persons (singular) : skill (singular)*, but this is a wonderful public space where many different behaviors occur simultaneously in a single scene, and can be observed at a single glance.

The above are patterns frequently observed, but there is something a little strange about your *a haircut by 9 hairdressers at once* and *a piano played by 5 pianists at once*. In the sense that a single work is created by multiple people, as shown by the title "a ~ by ~ s," for example, this fits into the matrix *persons (plural) : skill (singular)*.

Koki Tanaka:

We should think that open-source "wisdom of crowds" projects such as Wikipedia, where many people address the same subject, fit the matrix of *persons (plural) : skill (singular)*. On the other hand, I am not sure that the project of mine you have just mentioned could be placed in the same class. If we just look at the situation in the video documentation, it may seem to be *persons (plural) : skill (singular)*, but when we consider the total project, since an "author controlling the whole" is present on another level, I think there is a difference right there. It might be better to add the author's

position first as *person (singular)* → *persons (plural) : skill (singular)*. I, the author, set the framework of the piece. Even though, within this framework, several people make one thing, in the end the author claims the totality as a work. The situation in the video seems to be in the form you would expect, but the whole structure of the project is open to rather different interpretation. Nevertheless, the project is designed so that this layer of authorship may be removed, and then it essentially corresponds to your classification and expectations. In this project, if this individual "Author A" sets up the circumstances, the people participating in these circumstances are multiple "Authors a'" and, importantly, "Author A" does not control "Authors a'" but is at the disposal of "Authors a'."

YT:

So they depend on their own skills.

KT:

Yes, indeed, things simply take their course. I think that, if we keep to a methodology in which participants are allowed to do their own thing, then the privileging of "Author A" is reduced to some extent. Of course, some production methods such as making a feature film for example definitely need a "director" to control the situation. Others are

top: a haircut by 9 hairdressers at once (second attempt) (2010)
Material: HD video, Time: 28 min.
Credits: Commissioned by Yerba Buena Center for the Arts, San Francisco

bottom: a piano played by 5 pianists at once (first attempt) (2012)
Material: HD video, Time: 57 min.
Credits: Commissioned by University Art Galleries, UC Irvine,
Claire Trevor School of the Arts

Atelier Bow-Wow, *White Limousine Yatai* (2003)

needed, too, to divide various roles—actors, scriptwriters, camera operators, and so on—and the director will have the higher role of co-ordinating and integrating these people. Although a movie is produced by a large number of people, it is perceived in the end as a work with the director's name on it. In such cases, this is not collaboration in the sense that multiple participants are assigned roles to undertake a common task. It is rather a situation where an individual with an integrating identity subcontracts jobs. In an ideal collaboration, however, the positions of the participants are of equal value and a consensus is created. Of course it may be impossible for a project to move forward with the agreement and assent of all the participants.

Momoyo Kaijima:
In painting and sculpture, the Kano School and Rodin are in the pattern *person (singular) : skill (singular)*, aren't they.

KT:
Working as a large studio-like "factory," Takashi Murakami's production process, for example, is a pattern where *person (singular) : skill (singular)* integrates *persons (plural) : skill (singular)*. On the other hand,

in my recent series of projects, I have tried to record and examine whether co-operation rather than assigning a role is possible or, indeed, occasionally impossible. As far as I can do so, the positions of the people taking part are made the same. In the usual type of collaboration, roles are assigned spontaneously. Somebody takes the initiative, thereby creating a center or hierarchy. This perhaps is the limit of collaboration; and I am aware of something here. Previously I said in a self-critical way that the relationship between "Author A" and "Authors a'" shows a reduction in the privileging of "Author A" when things are left to go their own way, but another effect is that the positions of the participants are equal, due to the existence of "Author A." This equality of participants can only happen when "Author A" knows nothing about the skills of creation in which the participants are involved. In those projects, I was there as "Author A," who gave them a framework, but at the same time I was simply ignorant of what they were doing. In the presence of beauticians, poets, pianists, or potters, I have nothing to say about creative processes or methods. I know nothing about the skills in their fields, so I do not know how anything will be made, less so when the things were made in China. I didn't understand the language and could hardly have any exchanges with them. As the potters went ahead with their co-operative work I listened to bits of what they were saying, rendered into English by an interpreter, but I couldn't understand the entire process. What it amounts to is this: although I organize the situation, I'm the person that knows nothing about what's going on. Therefore, since I'm the person who is most peripheral to their process, the participants have to talk to each other and decide their own way forward. I make sure from the outset that they understand that they have to make up their own minds and if I were to be asked during the process how a piano piece should be composed, I would not have the slightest idea. Although the author has created the situation, he is absent.

YT:

Both architecture and film rely on an individual who has skills a, b, c, d, e, and so on, and other people with skills that are integrated by an individual with skill "a." By contrast, in a work by you, there are several people with the same skill and a person "a," who is without that skill and does not exert governance, so there is no role assignment. This is a state of equality only in that skills $a'=a''=a'''=a''''$ are shared. This may be termed commonality in a horizontal direction. *Person (singular) : skill (singular) → persons (plural) : skill (singular)* is a pyramid shape but *person (singular) : → persons (plural) : skill (singular)* is horizontal. This horizontal relationship is interesting. How did you arrive at it? Perhaps initially you were thinking about the identity of the author?

Something preceding the problem of community and antagonism

KT:

There is a widely held idea in Japan that an artwork is created by an impulse from within the author, but in my case, there is hardly any impulse welling up from within. And criticism about author-ship has long been held in contemporary art. There is a counter-movement against this, the idolization of the outsider or genius, someone with a strong individuality or authorship. I have the impression that this is particularly strong in Japan. But, nevertheless, it's impossible for me to be a powerful author with a powerful individuality. So what can a weak author with a meager individuality do?

For example, there is the book, *Relational Aesthetics* by Nicolas Bourriaud,[2] in which he sees in the activities of artists such as Liam Gillick and Rirkrit Tiravanija the idea of creating the site for a new relationship based on human interaction. They understand creativity as the discovery of a space where the emphasis is not on works as objects, but on human

Matrix for people and skills for the making
of a single [thing / site] (Ver. 1)

People Skills	Singular	Plural
Singular	Painting, sculpture (Integrating subject = individual)	White Limousine Yatai tai chi, ballroom dancing (Behavior sharing)
Plural	Self-build One-person performance	Architecture, films (role assigning) Joint performances

→ Multiple, simultaneous

interactions that are figuratively invisible. It seems that in the background to Bourriaud's formulation of this approach into a concept was the existence of Damien Hirst and the other so-called Young British Artists (YBAs): the YBAs came into prominence mainly in London, producing a group of market-friendly works that affirmed market values and art scene evaluations. By contrast, the forms of the works by the artists cited in *Relational Aesthetics* are indistinct. This seems to be unavoidable if it is remembered that human interactions are central. Also, there's so much collaboration that it's impossible to see what is whose work. Bourriaud understands and assesses the practices of these artists as something that parallels the development of the service industries in the post-Fordism era. Although this approach is twenty years old, it is still topical, and quite possibly we are still in this problematic area.

One thing that has remained unchanged is that, although the work might have been created by human relationships it is appraised as the work of a single artist, and so in the end the same problems of individuality and authorship as seen with the YBAs seem to lie in wait.

This was a trend of the 1990s and naturally enough it has come under some criticism since then. For instance, Claire Bishop in her article *Antagonism and Relational Aesthetics,*[3] poses the question that if human relationships are created, then quite what kind of relationships are they? Simply stated, all the people who participate in the projects of the artists dealt with by *Relational Aesthetics* are people with some relationship to art. Thus, what is happening seems to be that people gather with the clear purpose of looking at or participating in art, creating a scene much like a private view for an inner-circle community. Unless there is an encounter between communities that do not usually encounter each other, no antagonistic relationship will come about. This is a valid criticism: art practice is subjected to both appreciation and criticism when it adopts a certain kind of sociality. An antagonistic relationship should not be understood here as a negative thing. Antagonism is understood as an occasion for problems that are latent in a community to be brought to the surface. Although the claim in *Relational Aesthetics* is that new relationships are created, these are merely tepid relationships between colleagues. Bishop's criticism is that relationships should contain antagonism. Her argument is not without problems, however. For example, Bishop cites the projects of the Swiss artist Thomas Hirschhorn in her article. In 2002, he carried out the project *Bataille*

Monument in the poor, working-class area of the German town of Kassel. In 2013, he carried out a similar project, *Gramsci Monument Pavilion* in the Bronx, New York City. Both of these were in the kind of unsafe areas that the sort of people who would usually visit museums and galleries would be unlikely to stray. So, these projects functioned to bring together the kind of people who habitually go to view art with another community that they would not usually encounter in such a circumstance. And, of course, they also presented opportunities to hold workshops at temporary community centers, allowing the people of Kassel to encounter the thought of Georges Bataille and the people of the Bronx to encounter the thought of Antonio Gramsci. But this might seem somehow condescending and to label the locals as uneducated. It is also doubtful to what extent locals used the space. Although Bishop criticizes the works described in *Relational Aesthetics* as being just for an artistic inner circle, the artist's projects of which she seems to approve fall into the same situation. Just as the nature of the "relationships" poses a problem, the nature of the "antagonism" seems equally problematic.

The arguments of Bourriaud and Bishop should have been preconditions for the trends known as "participatory art" and "relational art" in Japan, but they gained acceptance with these parts removed. In Japan, the formal aspects and political nature of relational art have been bleached out and they are used as something politically convenient, for local revitalization or town planning. I am very critical of circumstances in which art is used as a tool of the administration.

YT:
So, functionality has been discovered in art.

KT:
To return to what we were talking about before, *Relational Aesthetics* has many more possibilities when we consider the problem of authorship. The problem I was examining here was people's participation, interaction, and process. For example, for *a haircut by 9 hairdressers at once (second attempt)*, the task of cutting a model's hair wasn't too difficult a task for nine hairstylists. After this piece, however, my consciousness shifted markedly towards the difficulty of collaborative making, and as the series was developed through *a piano played by 5 pianists at once (first attempt)* to *a poem written by 5 poets at once (first attempt)*, and *a pottery produced by 5 potters at once (silent attempt)*, it rapidly became more

top: a poem written by 5 poets at once (first attempt) (2013)
Material: HD video, Time: 68 min. 30 sec.
Credits: Commissioned by the Japan Foundation

bottom: a pottery produced by 5 potters at once (silent attempt) (2013)
Material: HD video, Time: 75 min.
Credits: Commissioned by the Japan Foundation
Created with Vitamin Creative Space, Guangzhou, and Pavilion, Beijing

top: Kitamoto Station West Plaza, Saitama Prefecture
bottom: Miyashita Park, Tokyo

complicated. In *a pottery produced by 5 potters at once (silent attempt)* each of the five participants was from a different background—one was a potter who held pottery workshops for children and parents in a city, another was an "artistic" potter who lived in the country and had even built his own kiln, and another was a contemporary potter who re-arranged existing pottery in her work and was also making a documentary film about ancient ceramic processes, and so on—so the difficulty manifested all the more. In the end, the framework disintegrated. One of the participants said that they didn't want to continue. Filming ended before the participants reached agreements on everything, with only some unfinished pots remaining. Thus, what was recorded was a failure of collaboration, which in the present context one could call a failure of the creation of commonality. I don't consider "failure" to be a negative, though. We always take too much notice of "correct-ness" and "success." One cannot ignore the fruitful experience inherent in failure.

MK:

When it comes to town planning, how-ever small the community, there's always some antagonism. In fact, it would be strange if there was no antagonism. People are quite aware of this and still go on living together. We were involved in the plan to renovate the Kitamoto Station West Plaza in 2013. There was a mayoral election during the project schedule and the people who were against the incumbent mayor also mounted a campaign against the project. In the end the mayor was re-elected, which meant the plan was endorsed indirectly, but it may well have been necessary for the community to have somewhere to fore-ground this problem through this expe-rience. Election campaigns become interesting and enjoyable events, when different opinions on a project are expressed. Miyashita Park wasn't a point of contention in the election even though some citizen groups and artists argued against it.

YT:

It was a scheme to renovate the dilapi-dated public park, funded by Nike Japan, as part of a naming-rights deal. There was a prerequisite from the start for another place in the park to be provided for the homeless, who have become more numerous since the collapse of the economic bubble around the mid-1990s. However, the people who supported the homeless regarded the project as one designed to throw them out. And a cam-paign to oppose the renovation started up because of this. It would have been better had we been provided more succinct information from the start. But it took two years for the town hall and Nike Japan to agree to the details and this caused excessive speculation. Eventually the park department (not the welfare department) of the town hall dealt with this carefully and courteously and persuaded the homeless people to move to the lower level of Miyashita Park.

KT:
Some of the people who were involved in the opposition to the Miyashita Park renovation understood the opposition movement as a form of self-expression. It's a question of the boundary between activist and artist although wider than the simple question of being for or against; it is part of the larger question about whether it's possible to practice social or political art in Japan. This is a point that interests me. I think there might be something there we should examine, something that is inseparable from those art projects that are exploited by the government. The musician Kenji Ozawa has been widely talked about, and in the UK, "community art" has been increasingly enlisted in policies and projects that contribute to the redevelopment or gentrification of certain areas, within a neoliberal context.

Opposition due to "commoning" that causes contention

KT:
If we use the matrix we were using before, I would think that the relationships that artists create are almost all *person (singular) : skill (singular) → persons (plural) : skill (singular)*. Whether this is an antagonistic relationship or a companionable club-like relationship, it is a predictable relationship created, "made," as it were, according to the image envisioned by the artist. This scope is hardly ever exceeded.

Next, I'll give my thoughts on this problem with reference to my own practice. In a sense, what I am conscious of in my practice is that the participants (including me, the person who sets it up) are placed in an uncertain situation in which the results cannot be predictable. To take the example of *a pottery produced by 5 potters at once (silent attempt)*, although the people I assembled had similar skills, they all had different backgrounds, and none of them readily found their common ground. In the process, from first encounter to collaboration, they had to convey to the other parties through words how they had previously created and based on which methods. The participants usually work alone or with assistants in some cases, but here, they had to work temporarily on a collaborative task with people they hardly knew. Accordingly, verbal explanations and communication were important elements. Of course they could also understand each other through actions. To demonstrate one's own skills is a form of communication. On the other hand, it was also possible that they were unable to communicate their beliefs. They were strangers after all, with very different ways of making and thinking. As they rubbed along together, a commonality became dimly evident in the situation. But, although something that they could share became evident, this did not mean that things necessarily went well. I think it is only when people are placed in these extremely uncertain circumstances that a possibility to create a kind of positive relationship is presented. However, this is almost always when participants are making something as in one of my projects. It could be that nothing is created by a haircut, but in the sense that they create a hairstyle, they may be described as artists. The fact that they were able to cope in a relatively open way with these short-term uncertain circumstances was perhaps because they were dealing with making in their own life. Something I noticed as I was filming was that the participants experienced completely different circumstances as part of a collaborative production, added to which was the video recording so that they were put in an extremely tense situation. Usually a project that aims for collaboration is carried out over a long period, of several months or even years. Here, however, they have to understand each other and make something over a relatively short time. So they were in a very pressurized situation. In order to share something with others one has to engage fully with the situation. So the participants became loquacious and were gradually driven to re-assess what they had previously done and what they had previously thought, including their methods. However, most people who happen to encounter people they do not know, and simply share a place and time with them, do not wish to engage fully. I think there is a rather risky and frightening aspect to sharing anything with a stranger—or commonality. The example of my work is one in which there is time-pressure and, I think, this is why this problem of commonality becomes more evident. In the end, do we really seek commonality? I think this also involves the possibility of people being forced into situations where individuality may break down.

MK:

Town planning, in the end, is about compromise. People may not understand each other but they have to live together and unless they give up on some things, they cannot make progress. On the other hand, it is the aesthetic sense that makes the final assessment in expressive media such as fine art. If this is so, I don't know whether a work is validated by evaluations in terms of commons and commonality.

YT:
Events such as piano performances and poetry recitations, which occur and disappear in real time, tend to succeed easily because ad libbing is effective. A hairdo, however, becomes increasingly difficult as the hair left to cut becomes less and less. Potting is even more difficult. The authorship of a ceramic piece manifests in the integral accumulation of continuous working, by hand, of the clay directly in front of the potter, the contours of the object, and the feedback from this. If a stranger becomes mixed in with this, behaving in the same way as oneself, the feedback from the clay is overwritten from the start.

On the other hand, the behaviors we are talking about, here, such as drinking and eating under cherry trees when they are blossoming and being able to use chairs to sit and face each other when having a chat, are behaviors without authorship. If such behaviors are gathered together and monopolize a certain time and space, these behaviors are shared. This is one condition for thinking about the character of public space.

Matrix for people and skills for the making of a single [thing / site] (Ver. 2)

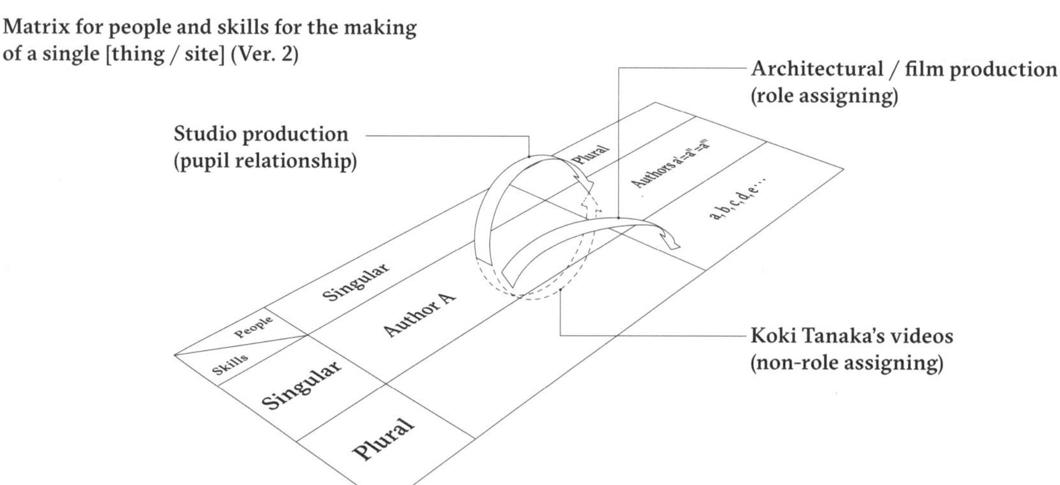

David Harvey uses the word 'commoning' in an argument concerning the use of places within which many subjects exist.[4] Antagonism occurs when commoning takes place; that is, when an attempt is made to imbue a place with common norms. This argument describes both a form of commoning in which the site used is free of the selfish interests of others and another form, commoning as viewed by commerce, in which commercial capital uses the space for profit. In both cases, a domain that is not commercial capital is imbued with norms. The problem, however, is that when there is competition between these types of commoning, it is considered inevitable for commercial capital to prevail. This tone, which has not only been adopted by the media, has also become established in people's minds so that there is a risk of a division into two extremes—a feeling of powerlessness and ideological revolt—rather than arguments about specific cases.

The relationship between contextual re-reading and making

KT:
There is, I think, a type of thinking about commonality in our everyday that we re-read. In considering this, I shall take the example of a work with "behavior" in the title: *a behavioral statement (or an unconscious protest)*, as exhibited in the Japanese Pavilion at the 55th Venice

Co-operation without role-assigning
(horizontal relationship)

The privileging of "Author A" is
weakened by lack of governance;
to be equal in status to the participants

Role-assigning co-operation
(pyramid relationship)

"Author A" integrates
plural people × plural skills

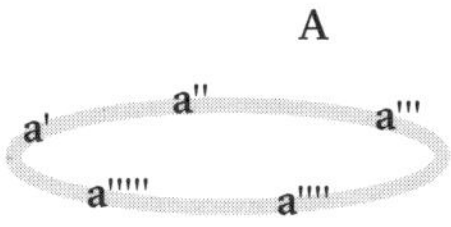

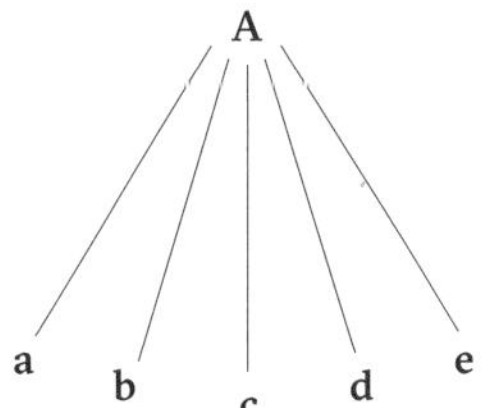

Biennale in 2013. This is an image of many people ascending and descending an emergency stairway.

As I am based in Los Angeles, I was in a position where I could not take part in the antinuclear demonstrations even though I agreed with them. There may have been people in the distant regions of Japan that felt the same way. So I changed the way I looked at it: What does it mean to participate, and are there not other ways of participating? I thought that I might be able to find some form of antinuclear gesture in everyday behavior that would allow me to transcend this distance and take part in the antinuclear demonstration. One of the circumstances I noticed in Tokyo during a short visit to Japan was during a scheduled power cut to reduce electricity after damage to the Fukushima nuclear power plant following the tsunami of 2011. The station escalators were halted and people used the stairs. I thought that this behavior of using the stairs, of which they were unconscious, or, rather, which they neither opposed nor assented to, could itself be re-read as an antinuclear gesture. I thought that if the everyday behavior of "ascending and descending stairs" in itself could be perceived as the antinuclear protest, our consciousness could be changed in the everyday. In *a behavioral statement (or an unconscious protest)*, the group ascending the stairs and the group descending the stairs mingle with each other as they go in opposite directions. If there was only the group descending the stairs, this might be understood as representing an image of the evacuation after the disaster. But there is also the group ascending the stairs. Here, as the two groups mix, there is a gradation of opinions, in contrast to the situation in contemporary Japan post-Fukushima, where there is a clear choice between opposition to and support of nuclear power, and this reflects the question of whether there could be something less black-and-white—a grey opinion. I have chosen an action in which, although there was exactly the same behavior in society before and after the earthquake, the significance of the behavior has changed by a re-reading, due to a change of context. Because we have ascended and descended stairs both before and after the earthquake.

I think that re-reading the context is an important feature of the previous activities of Atelier Bow-Wow. It is an attitude in which, by researching cities, the structures of buildings and cities, which we tend to overlook are re-read. When I consider the relationship between the re-reading of the context and the creation of buildings, I realize how wonderful architecture is. In re-reading

a behavioral statement (or an unconscious protest) (2013)
Material: HD video, Time: 8 min.
Credits: Commissioned by the Japan Foundation
Equipment support: ARTISTS' GUILD
Production photograph: Takashi Fujikawa

the context based on its research, we discover the possibilities of architecture by adjusting and repositioning the context of all those many things in the city that have deviated from and gone beyond their initial purposes and functions. When designing a building, doesn't one have to create a place with some degree of purpose, however loose this might be? For example, one cannot create a location that is a dance studio and also a diner-kitchen, nor a place that is both a grave-yard and a nursery school. In that sense, even when a design aims to bring variety to a space, it is not possible to bundle more than two or three possibilities together. Perhaps one can only leave it up to the users' creativity. What research into cities shows is that probably while the bundling of possibilities should be very wide it is likely to be narrowed at the design stage. I may be naïve, but I believe this is why architects can make something that has purpose in a place where people's creativity can dismiss the given purpose and even open up other possibilities. On the other hand, I have the impression that the bundle of possibilities in projects where a relational situation is made, such as in *White Limousine Yatai*, is wider in

Atelier Bow-Wow, Ikushima Library, Tokyo (2008)

scope than in architectural design. And that is precisely why I think that Atelier Bow-Wow is dealing with public spaces and people's interaction where the bundle of possibilities might be wider.

YT:
The reason that the bundle of possibilities seems narrow is that we are restricted in the types of relationships we use. But having a purpose is also one of the fascinations of architecture. By having a purpose, one may pose the question: Why, here and now, is architecture necessary for these people? This question brings to light the interlinking of the various things on which the architecture is established. Since a range of factors, including nature, science, engineering, culture, history, society, and the economy, is contained in this interlinkage, the bundle of relationships is very wide. By re-reading and re-combining this interlinkage, the purposes of architecture, which has been reaching exhaustion, is liberated in a direction that is filled with life.

**Salvation brought about
by sharing behavior**

MK:
I think that systems and regulations

form a mechanism that brings about better architecture, but I also think that it is a problem that all of society is involved in this mechanism and is moving in a direction that precludes any escape from it. Since architecture is something that creates places where people live, I think it should help people to relax but, in fact, there are more and more cases where architecture controls people. In order to escape this, it is necessary to study this mechanism, return it to its original meaning and excavate the poetic force towards which the space and architecture were aiming, and thus discover a different topology. This is difficult, but is the fascination of architecture.

KT:
Returning to Tokyo after some time, I noticed one particular behavior: there was a powerful obsession with social rules among people on trains. And beyond that, some people reacted excessively against them. For example, an elderly woman sat down on one of the priority seats reserved for the elderly and disabled and, noticing a man in his thirties also sitting on one of these seats, shouted angrily, "This is a priority seat. You should follow social rules." I understand how the woman felt, but since she had only happened to sit on a priority seat, there was nobody else who needed

one, and the train was not very crowded, I thought she could have left it alone. The man she addressed responded with a terse "Right," and just sat there stubbornly, showing no signs of getting up, and remaining in place after the woman got off. Both reactions were obsessive and I found them rather disturbing.

YT:

At the time when behaviorism—which observed behavior and emphasized the relationship between stimulus and response—was incorporated into architectural planning, it was thought that human behavior could be controlled as a mechanistic response to the physical environment, but I have heard that this was also much criticized. The recent environment-controlled architecture is in that tradition. In our behaviorology, first, the subjects of behaviors are not limited to people; they include, more widely, natural elements and physical objects such as architecture; we also focus on the fact that those enacting the behaviors have the power to control them. Thus, a range of actors behaves compliantly and aims to achieve equilibrium. Individuals cannot therefore monopolize the term behavior. The behavior of nature obeys natural laws and natural providence. The behaviors of people living in a certain society and culture are internalized as skills and may also be described as an open resource that can be studied. If people learn a behavior there will be many places where they can participate in it, but the site for their behavior can be created as well as canceled. Thus, even when services are not provided, there is still some room for people to be able use their own initiative. We wish to create architecture and public spaces in a direction that will encourage this. Our aim is architectural design in which the emphasis is shifted from individuality to commonality.

1   Koki Tanaka, *abstract speaking—
sharing uncertainty and collective acts*,
Japanese Pavilion, 55th Venice Biennale
(June 1–November 24, 2013).

2   Nicolas Bourriaud, *L'esthétique relationelle*
(Paris: Les Presses du Réelle, 1998);
Relational Aesthetics, tr. Simon Pleassance
and Fronz Woods (Paris: Les Presses
du Réelle, 2002).

3   Claire Bishop, "Antagonism and Relational
Aesthetics," *October*, 110 (fall 2004): 51–79.

4   David Harvey, *Rebel Cities: From the
Right to the City to the Urban Revolution*
(London: Verso, 2013).

The Production of Behavior and Conditions for People to Live in a Town

In the chapter "Commonalities of Architecture," people's behavior was cited as one of the common resources that could be described as the bases of commonality, and public spaces identified as areas of spatial design which develop from this. We have encountered and observed practice of this kind of design throughout the world. We have learned much from the behaviors of people in urban spaces and we will describe some of these behaviors below. Before starting on these individual reports, we will describe the conditions for these behaviors by people, the background to our discussion of these, the framework that encompasses these, and also the possibility of linking these to the design of public space.

What we have focused on is the behaviors of people that characterize a town, the unremunerated, multiple, reiterated behaviors performed by the public at places in the town where others can observe them. These behaviors are neither specific behaviors nor special amusements. They are behaviors performed everyday, in a daily or weekly rhythm, by the people of the neighborhood without being particularly conscious of them. Consequently, a festival held at an annual rhythm cannot be one of these. A festival belongs to the class of unusual events (festival preparations on the other hand may be usual and included in these behaviors). Above all, these are the autonomous behaviors of people, reiterated and transcending subjectivities. Unlike behaviors performed at a facility (such as at a school, library, or art gallery) created for the purpose, these do not constitute the basic purpose for which the place was created. And this is why they are difficult to understand from within the system of architecture, which is organized around the making of buildings. But this may be precisely why they have continued to exist without incorporating the "biopower" which has expanded particularly in the latter half of the twentieth century.

As described by Michel Foucault, "biopower"—a system that emerged in place of the ruler's "right to kill"—is a system that manages and controls people through structures that enhance their lives. Characteristically, since it enhances lives, it is impervious to criticism and since it is not oppressive, it may not seem like power at all. This new power has proved most radical in the field of health—in that people are alive and the state has a responsibility for their health—but it also penetrates the construction sector. Therefore, standards are provided for social infrastructures and construction, and production systems are managed by specialists and validated by an academic framework and a schema in which the enviromentalization of biopower is promoted by a construction industry and is assembled by industry, bureaucracy, and academia. As this schema spreads throughout the entire society it seems likely that people's behaviors will become increasingly disciplined. To divert a little, let us consider the example of the sea-flood protection planned for the sites of the 2011 Tōhoku earthquake and tsunami. The schema that accompanied this dictates that the height of the new sea defenses was calculated by a decision of the government, mobilizing the science of simulation, on the basis that the state maintains the safety of the people, and the design and construction were granted renewal aid and this in turn will have an economic effect. The problem is not just that that the sea defenses are so high that the sea is no longer visible from the land. This schema is a hybrid of politics, science, engineering, and economics, as described by the sociologist of science Bruno Latour, and other choices are repelled. These choices include the previous way of life of the local residents, in which they organized their lives so that they lived and worked where they could see the ocean, could rapidly detect any hazard, and immediately connect this to evacuation. When the new sea defenses are complete, some of the behaviors previously embedded in that way of life, with that view of the sea, may well not return.

The opinion that safety comes first is to be expected; also the plan has the attraction that investment is made locally. A concerning aspect, however, is that this creates people who, although living on a tsunami-prone ria coastline, do not know how to protect themselves from the risk of a tsunami. And despite the fact that this may well pose a higher probability of a risk in the future.

Thus, the biopower system does not address people's behaviors directly, but in the end, it has the tendency to enclose, and constrain, people's behaviors by piling up several layers of logic for the people's benefit. At the same time, the bonds between people produced by joint ownership of autonomous behaviors, where they think and act for themselves, are broken. This is a degradation of commonality. And when this is so, conversely, the power of mutual aid does not engage during a disaster or other emergency, as has been pointed out for a range of aspects. Another danger that has been described is that individuals with no common ground, who are also divided off from the government and the totality, are picked off and stripped bare by the logic of neoliberalism which, sheltering behind the universality of the market, recognizes no choice other than free competition. A framework used to comprehend behaviors must answer the question of how to address this problem.

Accordingly, we shall try considering people's behavior as something that is produced. If people's behavior is reiterated in transcendence of subjects, this is because there is at least something like a production line. The mode of action of the "biopower" system is that it does not address behaviors but continually addresses society, nature, culture, and the economy, narrowing the permitted range of behaviors, and increasingly remaking them into things where no autonomy can be exerted. This being so, then, conversely, the relationship between society, and nature, culture, and economics, which produce behaviors, should be examined from the point of view of behaviors, by directly addressing behaviors with autonomy. Within this framework, it should be possible to protect and expand autonomous behavior by the containment of people's behaviors.

Not, of course, that this will be understood from the very beginning. Rather, a framework that gradually draws out the possibilities of behaviors that seem interesting may emerge as these observations continue. The relationship between behaviors and the various elements that constitute this framework will be examined from first principles.

The least dispensable thing for human behavior is the body. A body has size and nobody else can occupy the space occupied by the body. On the other hand, the body has inbuilt physical abilities (skills) not apparent from its appearance. These skills can be learned from others and refined by repetition so that they become part of the body. There has to be a certain space around the body for these skills to be exercised. Therefore, through a general agreement by all those with such skills, places where these skills can be demonstrated are produced in sizes and densities that accord to the types of skill. For example, groups of people assemble early each morning along the promenade of the Bund in Shanghai to take exercise. There are people practicing tai chi as well as ballroom dancing, doing aerobics to music, kite flying, walking backwards, and all the many other ways that people choose to keep fit. Circles of friends chat and clusters of enthusiasts evolve, with the space between these individuals dictated by the particular form of activity. Thus, an interior is formed by a common physical skill, and feelings of belonging to these interiors fill the area. This is an appropriation of the space. Moreover, in that there are no physical enclosures, the behaviors of neighboring clusters resemble the behaviors of boats on the river and the behaviors of cars and bicycles on the road. Thus, a single flat area of the promenade is changed into a lively public space in which multiple intimate spaces are arrayed.

This can be described as resembling children playing in a town: hide-and-seek, baseball on the street, soccer in a square, skateboarding on the steps. The basic skills are immanent in the body, provided there is the necessary minimum of equipment and companions, a large enough area, and a place where safety is assured can always be found. However, towns were not designed for the playing of sport and the rules have to be modified to some extent to suit the place, but this does not interfere with the children playing and imagining their sporting idols. The example of the Shanghai Bund, however, only shows that with increasing age such play begins to take into account sociality and that it can still be regarded as playing with friends. The more one owns public space through physical skill, and changes it into one's own space, the greater is the pleasure of play.

Something else that is indispensable for people's behavior is the behavior of nature. For example, cleaning and other work in which the body is used is a behavior that is reiterated and can be described as a behavior of people into which an element of nature has been introduced. In the older residential areas of Tokyo, where hedges and trees still surround rows of large detached houses, one may observe the figures of those sweeping up fallen leaves. This occurs daily in the autumn and winter when there are many falling leaves. Leaves, which are not seen as litter when they fall on earth, change into rubbish when they fall on asphalt. On occasion, over-enthusiastic people pursue the leaves so far that they finish sweeping them up in front of somebody else's house. This, however, might be unwanted interference in a neighbor's affairs and the person in the house whose front is swept in this way may feel some shame. The anxiety arising from this is caused by the existence of property boundaries. Thus there are: the leaf-sweeping behavior, including the attendant worry; the meteorological behavior that is the change of seasons; the leaves and the wind that are behaviors of nature; the road which makes the leaves look like rubbish; the broom that is the equipment for brushing them up; and the property bound-aries, which cause the people anxiety about whether this behavior is some form of boundary infringement. The behaviors of leaf-sweeping are produced when a living and breathing body is placed where these interlink. Conversely, the behaviors of leaf-sweeping interlink elements in different dimensions.

Leaf-sweeping is a finite task that can be completed but the tending of plants and trees is a continuous task in which people engage together producing co-operative behaviors. In the South Korean City of Kwangju, for example, green chilies and sesame plants are grown in every possible place, not only on small areas of spare ground produced by road alterations and the man-made slopes joining the road and building plots on different levels; green chilies and sesame plants flourish in old water troughs left by the roadside and polystyrene boxes on balconies. These urban farms have in common the food culture of South Korea, the memory of Kwangju's agricultural past, and the background of the crowded buildings of the residential area. Conversely, through this behavior, a relationship is established between specific plants, the sun, seasons, house rebuilding, and, on occasion, sizable pieces of refuse.

Green chilies and sesame plants are elements of nature, but they are cooked or processed to become edible. Cooking and processing combine ingredients available from various sites to make them enjoyable to eat or to give them a longer storage life. This is the culture of everyday life. Let us now consider a behavior that connects music and musical instruments to food and processed products.

As an example, in Dublin one Sunday evening, people drinking in a pub suddenly begin to play music. The pub staff says nothing. The other customers sitting at the same tables with the musicians continue to drink their beer. Mixed with the familiar instruments of violin, flute, recorder, guitar, and accordion is an instrument like small bagpipes (the Uillean pipes) and what looks like a large tambourine (bodhrán). They perform Irish folk songs with great accomplishment. Noticing that during their performance they ask each other if they know a particular tune, we suppose that they do not all belong to the same band. Their performing skills have been polished by constant repetition so that they sound both accomplished and agreeable. This is the regular Sunday "session" at this pub, music making by customers for the pleasure of it, unscheduled by any management. Accordingly, no payment is made either for the performance or for the use of the pub. A behavior, the session, is produced in which Irish folk songs, a cultural resource built up through the history of the region, is the platform, and beer the lubricant, and multiple subjects participate in a demonstration of the skill of musical performance. This also demonstrates the general welcome offered by the pub (the public house), a place where performers, non-performers, and tourists could all be together. It was clear from the confident,

Kwangju, South Korea: green chilies and
sesame plants grow in every possible place.

cheerful expressions of those performing in the pub that for the people living in this area, the session was undoubtedly a part of their cultural identity. The music is close to the people, their common property, and autonomous. It was obvious that this manifests as a commonality, which strengthens the bonds joining the people. Unlike the other examples, this session was not observed in an external space, but despite the fact that it was an extension of the eating and drinking that is the function of the pub, it is a behavior that links to a socially and culturally deeper stratum, and thus is described as an example performed in a public place.

In comparison with this, it is astonishing how intensely the musical environment that surrounds us has been industrialized. If we wish to choose music to listen to, we buy it; if we want to sing, then we pay for karaoke. We have a huge range of choices but usually nobody near us knows which songs we like to hear or sing. In an industrialized musical environment, pieces of music manifest as things that separate individuals and the relationship is passive and highly dependent on the commercial system. Perhaps, like the people of Vietnam during their resistance to the attacks of the USA, at the critical moment, a song may yet emerge from deep within us.

Vehicles and buildings, and other structures, are essential for a grasp of people's behaviors in towns. We could also discuss the complex of the behaviors of nature and the weather and people's behaviors here, but will leave this to a later section and instead present a summary of our claims. That is, people's behaviors are produced. There is something like a production line for specific behaviors in the town and the repetition of behaviors transcending differences in subjects is established through the relationship of this with living and breathing bodies. This production line is composed of the reciprocal relationships between the behaviors of climate and nature, things such as tools and vehicles, cultural skills such as sports, music, and cuisine, and the social infrastructure, and buildings, and so on, where these are located. Conversely, behaviors link things belonging to different dimensions. Therefore, by addressing the behaviors that characterize the town, one should be able to comprehend these reciprocal relationships in terms of behaviors. Finding the mutual relationships of things is linked with the unpicking of the relationships between nature, society, culture, and environment, the conditions under which people live in towns.

It can be said that the places where typical behaviors are produced spontaneously from these reciprocal relationships and the people who perform them are also characterized by the production of these behaviors. The reciprocal dependency of place and behaviors is sometimes termed "place identity." We find in these reciprocal relationships of things linked together by behaviors the opportunity to direct architectural design not toward "a totality as the sum of quantifiable individuals" but toward "a totality as a bundle of relationships between things." The reconstruction of this latter totality is of the greatest importance; its loss is linked to the current fragmentation of daily life, particularly in urban areas. This fragmentation is being accelerated by the endemic industrialization that surrounds daily life, from clothing, food, and housing to music. Architecture has also played a significant part in this. The rhetoric that claims that a widening of choice means an increase in free will is widely believed. Attention to people's behavior relativizes this rhetoric and liberates the possibilities of co-ownership and commonality from the distant corner into which they have been driven. Thus, to think in terms of behavior is an effective means of shifting the emphasis of architectural practice from "individuality" to "commonality."

However, architectural design cannot be directly in contact with behavior. This is because behavior is within the people's domain. What can be done is to intervene in the production line of behaviors, as described above, to understand the reciprocal relationships between things and continue this review so that it is linked with a more certain reconstruction of the totality. Based on this premise, when importance is placed on commonality, the design of public space and the provision of physical facilities, with society's agreement, will take a direction which is rich in the reciprocal relationships of things and in which the autonomous behaviors of people are consistently repeatable.

The chairs at the Luxembourg Gardens
Luxembourg Gardens, Paris, France
Chairs recording people's behaviors

Chairs that record people's behavior

Using two chairs while reading

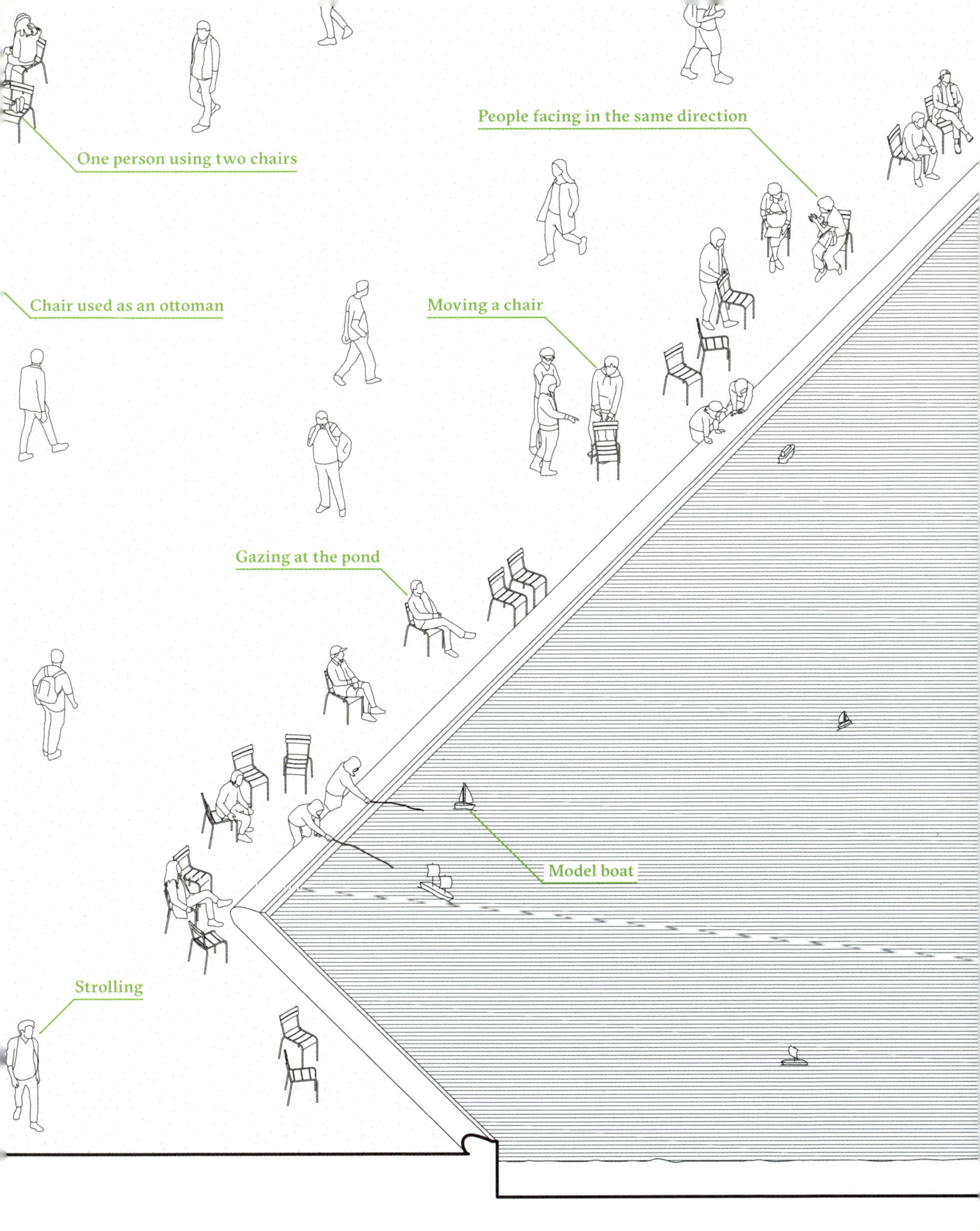

One person using two chairs
People facing in the same direction
Chair used as an ottoman
Moving a chair
Gazing at the pond
Model boat
Strolling

There is a host of iron chairs, painted deep green, placed in the Luxembourg Gardens in Paris. They are just light enough for an adult to pick up with one hand and can be taken anywhere in the Gardens and used as the person wishes. One person has parked a chair near a pond and is enjoying a tanning session both from direct sunlight and from the light reflected from the water. Another has arranged two chairs so that they face each other, has stretched out his legs as if on an ottoman and is snoozing. Another person has taken a chair to the foot of a tree and is reading in the shade. Yet others are sitting in a circle and chatting. There are many behaviors in the Gardens and most of them are produced by the use of the chairs in the Garden environment. The behaviors produced by the chairs are not only those of their living and breathing occupants. The forms of three people chatting seem to hover over the three empty chairs facing each other. This behavior is side by side with the behavior of the living. Since the chairs are not fixed, we were concerned that some characters might take them home with them, but, apparently, they are not taken out of the Garden. People know how these chairs should be treated and share common standards regarding them, and taking them away would be regarded harshly as something that would wound the Parisian's pride. In that sense, too, this is a wonderful invention. These chairs were introduced by the Paris Parks Department in 1923 and are to be found also in the Palais-Royal.

Chairs arranged exactly as people want them. →
Chairs recording people's behaviors.

"Bearpit Karaoke Show" in Mauerpark
Mauerpark, Berlin, Germany
Songs fill a hollow in the ground

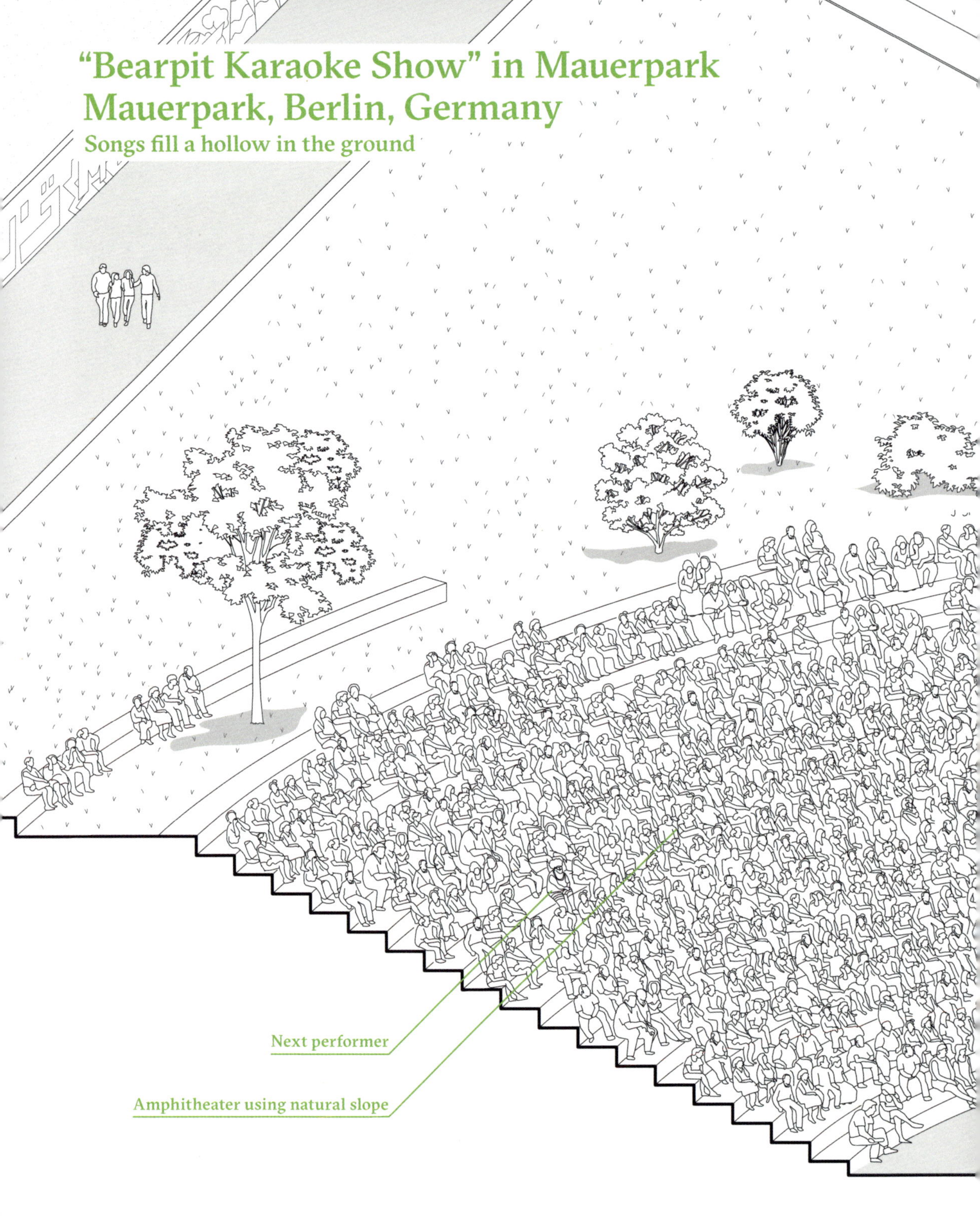

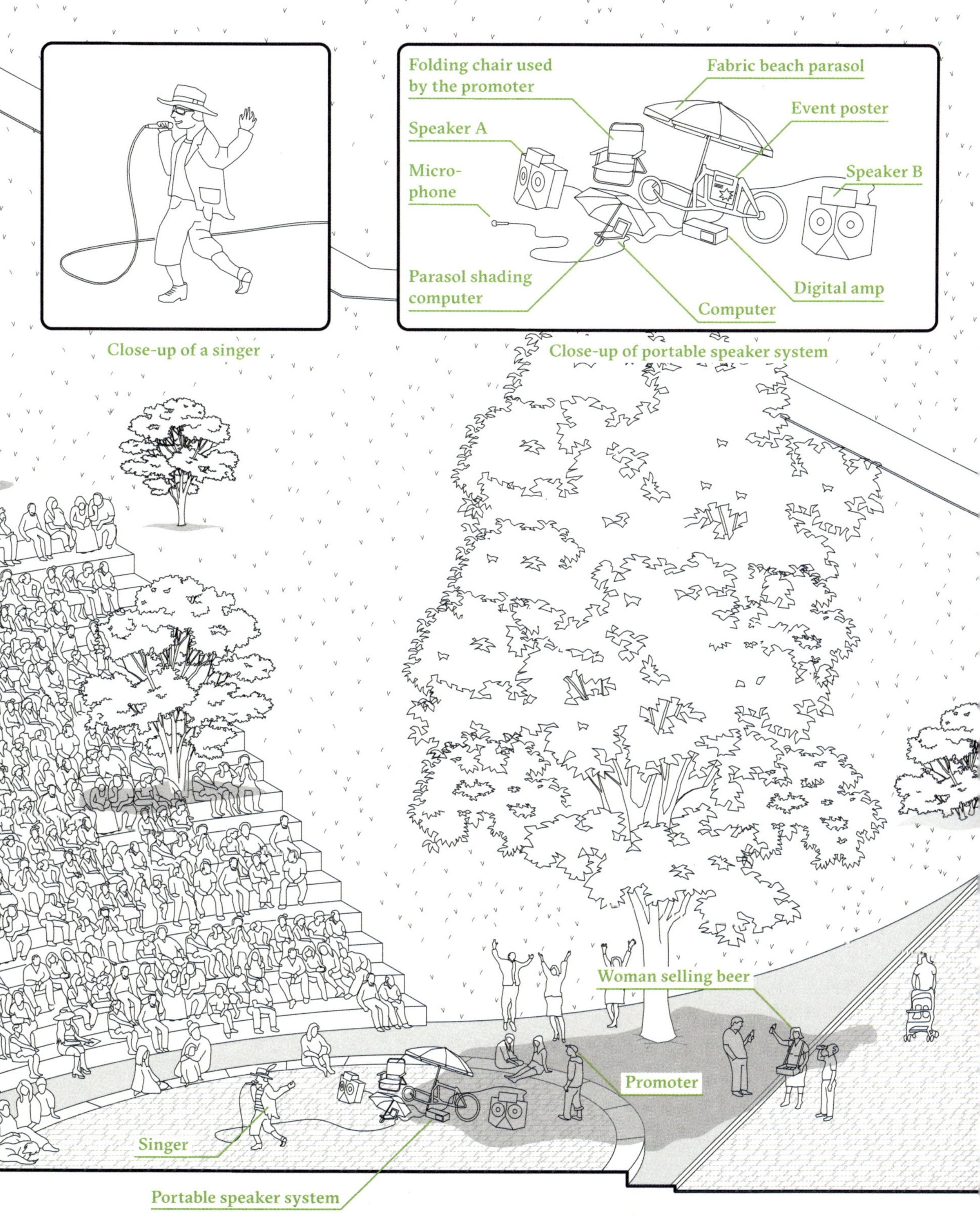
Close-up of a singer
Folding chair used by the promoter
Fabric beach parasol
Speaker A
Event poster
Micro-phone
Speaker B
Parasol shading computer
Digital amp
Computer
Close-up of portable speaker system
Woman selling beer
Promoter
Singer
Portable speaker system

One weekend in Berlin, having heard there was a flea market, we set out for Mauerpark. In a large field scattered with trees there were rows of simple wooden stalls selling old clothes, old records, old furniture, and the like. Passing by these, we came out into a wide field. Here were many Turkish people gathered into extended family groups and enjoying barbecues. There was an amphitheater, using the topography of the slope up to a sports stadium to the east, with a full audience. There was a single singer on the stage and a man behind operating a small machine. When the song finished, this man took the microphone and called somebody's name. Someone in the audience put up their hand and came down to take the singer's place. Different music started and another song began. It was clear that this was an amateur karaoke concert. What was impressive was the audience's warm reception. Even when the singer was not very good they were encouraged with applause, and good singers were cheered. The audience enjoyed not only the singers' talent and their outfits, but also the character of singer, the selection of songs and the fact that they were rocking the place together. As the amphitheater faced west, the sun reached in until the end of the concert.

From what we heard, the karaoke concerts, which began in 2009, have become an established free event from 3 p.m. each Sunday. The organizer is Joe Hatchiban, from Dublin, and people who want to sing book ahead on the internet. Joe prepares the day's songs on a computer and, on the day, arrives at the park on a bicycle adapted to be a sound system. At first, he sings himself and then he calls the names of those who have booked and then plays the karaoke backing. His intention is to produce a venue where people gather who would usually be in completely different social positions. Occasionally, middle-aged women selling beer appear to serve the audience, which may be more than a thousand people. Recently, Coca-Cola has become a sponsor.

Mauerpark, a park and other facilities created from the no-man's land on each side of the Berlin Wall after its fall in 1989, also has the special feature of having an exhibition where it is possible to learn the many tales about the Wall at the very place these tales were created.

The audience fill the amphitheater. People who
have booked to sing go down to the stage when
their name is called.

Morning at the Temple of Heaven, in front of the Eastern Gate
Temple of Heaven, Beijing, China
Possession of space by various personal exercises

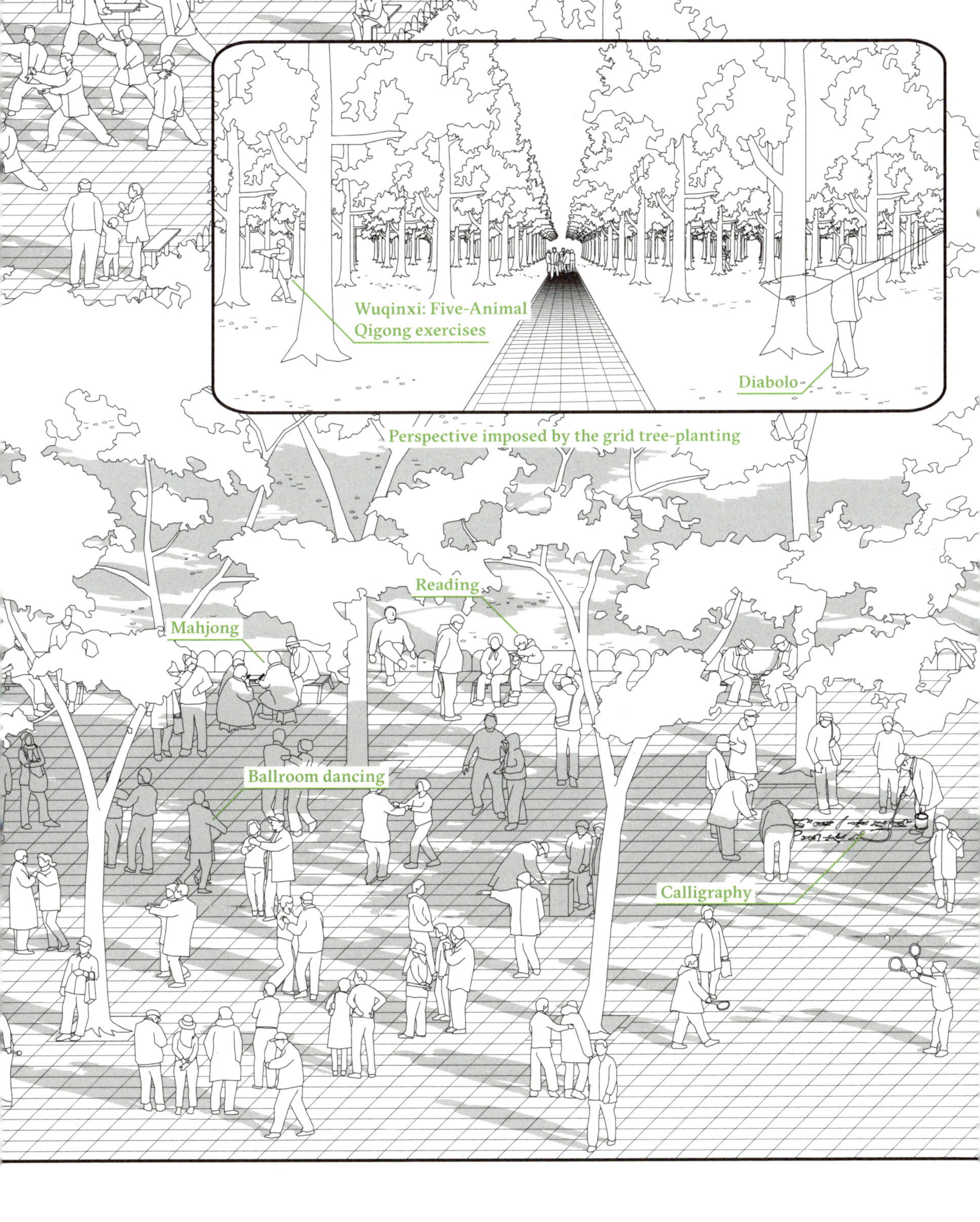

Wuqinxi: Five-Animal Qigong exercises
Diabolo
Perspective imposed by the grid tree-planting
Reading
Mahjong
Ballroom dancing
Calligraphy

Beijing, the Temple of Heaven Park, 6 a.m. From various places in the pitch-dark park come strange calls of "Ho-ho!" There are people walking backwards round the stone pavement of the platform that forms the central axis of the park. At the facing South Gate, someone is walking backwards up and down the surrounding slope and another is pressing the pressure points of his shoulders against the head of one of the large nails in the door. As our eyes become accustomed to the dusk and the sky lightens, we find ourselves in the midst of an extensive forest. The park is planted with oaks and other trees in a grid pattern at intervals of six or seven meters and this opens up forwards, sideways, and at oblique perspectives. A slowly moving figure becomes visible a hundred meters ahead; a person passes straight by walking backwards. Everywhere there are glimpses of people in the shade of the trees carrying out their own favorite type of exercise. We knew that the slow movements are a part of tai chi but everything else we see is new to us. One person presses the pressure points of his back against the knots of an old tree, another slides her fingers up the trunk of a tree and rubs her entire palms down it again. There is a group exercising while reciting sutras, people playing something like battledore and shuttlecock, another operates a humming spinning top with a cord attached to a stick, another flies a kite, another flourishes a whip, there is a group street dancing, another person practices styles of swordplay, young women do aerobic exercises to pop music. In the Long Corridor, a group hurls weighted spinning tops high into the air, another group sits on the verandah to play cards, a choir sings. Some people use large brushes to write out poems in water on the stone pavement. All have discovered and are carrying out their own personal fitness regimes.

This imposing garden, created in the late fifteenth century for the Ming and Qing emperors to pray for good harvests is now busy every morning, mainly with middle-aged and older men and women. Since dying trees are replaced with new ones, young saplings less than ten years old stand next to ancient trees with a history of three centuries. The grid of trees creates a large volume of transparent "rooms" without walls in the park. This scene, in which a vast range of people's behaviors coincides and overlaps, resembles a picture scroll. It is said, that, in the background to this rich fitness culture are health-promotion policies, including the simplification of tai chi by the

top left:
An accomplished performer almost balletically keeps a shuttlecock in the air.

top right:
Tai chi practice between the trees

middle left:
Calligraphy with water

middle right:
Tai chi at the Long Corridor

bottom left:
Tai chi Swords

bottom right:
Tai chi softball;
a combination of badminton and taichi

government in the 1950s, but there is little sign of a bond between these people and the state. To master one's own technique is a fine thing. If, however, social customs change with the astonishing economic growth and the society becomes one where the environment is controlled, it may be that people's habits will be constrained as they adapt to this environment. As generations change, will the Chinese people be able to maintain bodies that produce such spatial performances?

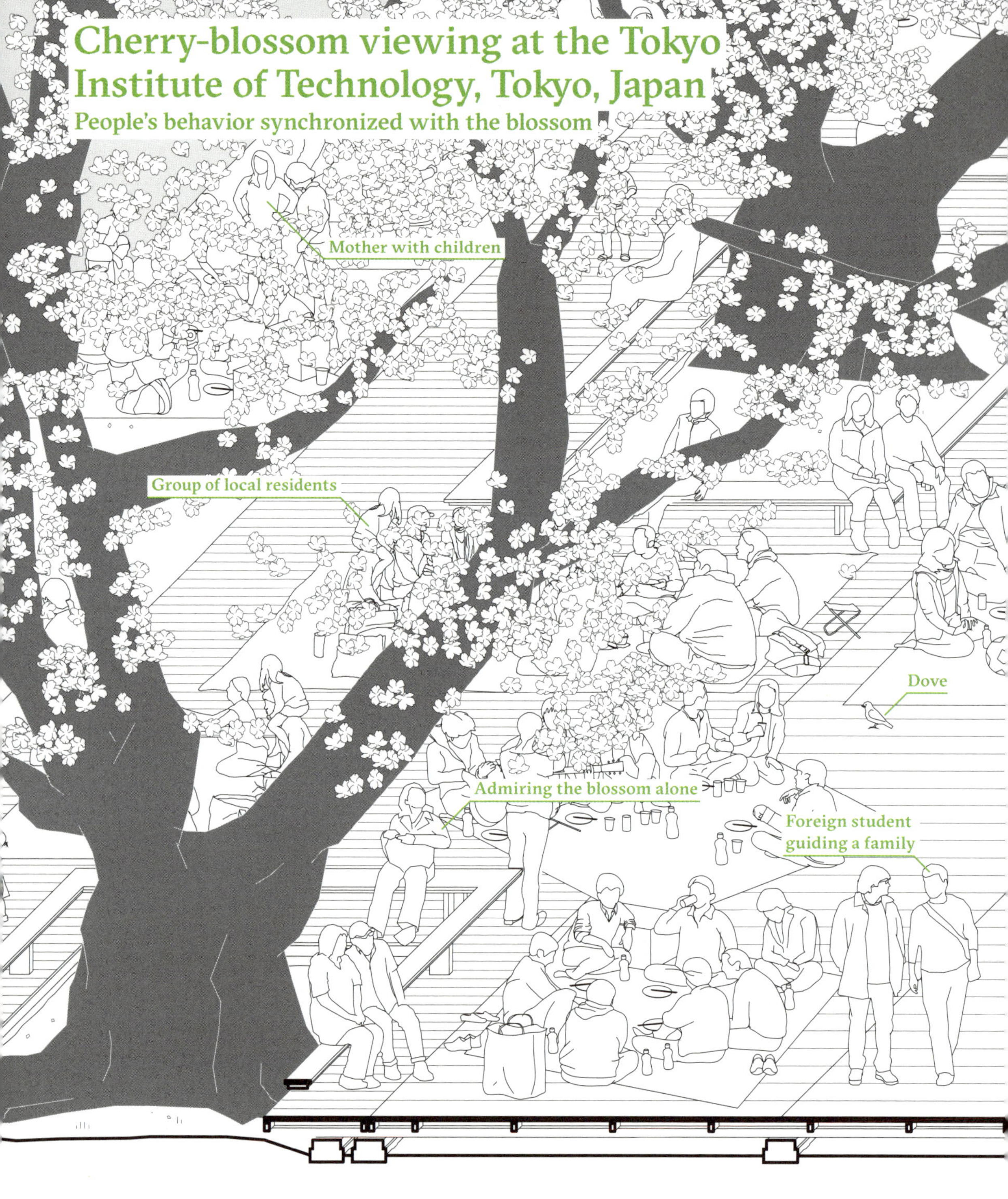

Cherry-blossom viewing at the Tokyo Institute of Technology, Tokyo, Japan
People's behavior synchronized with the blossom
Mother with children
Group of local residents
Admiring the blossom alone
Dove
Foreign student guiding a family

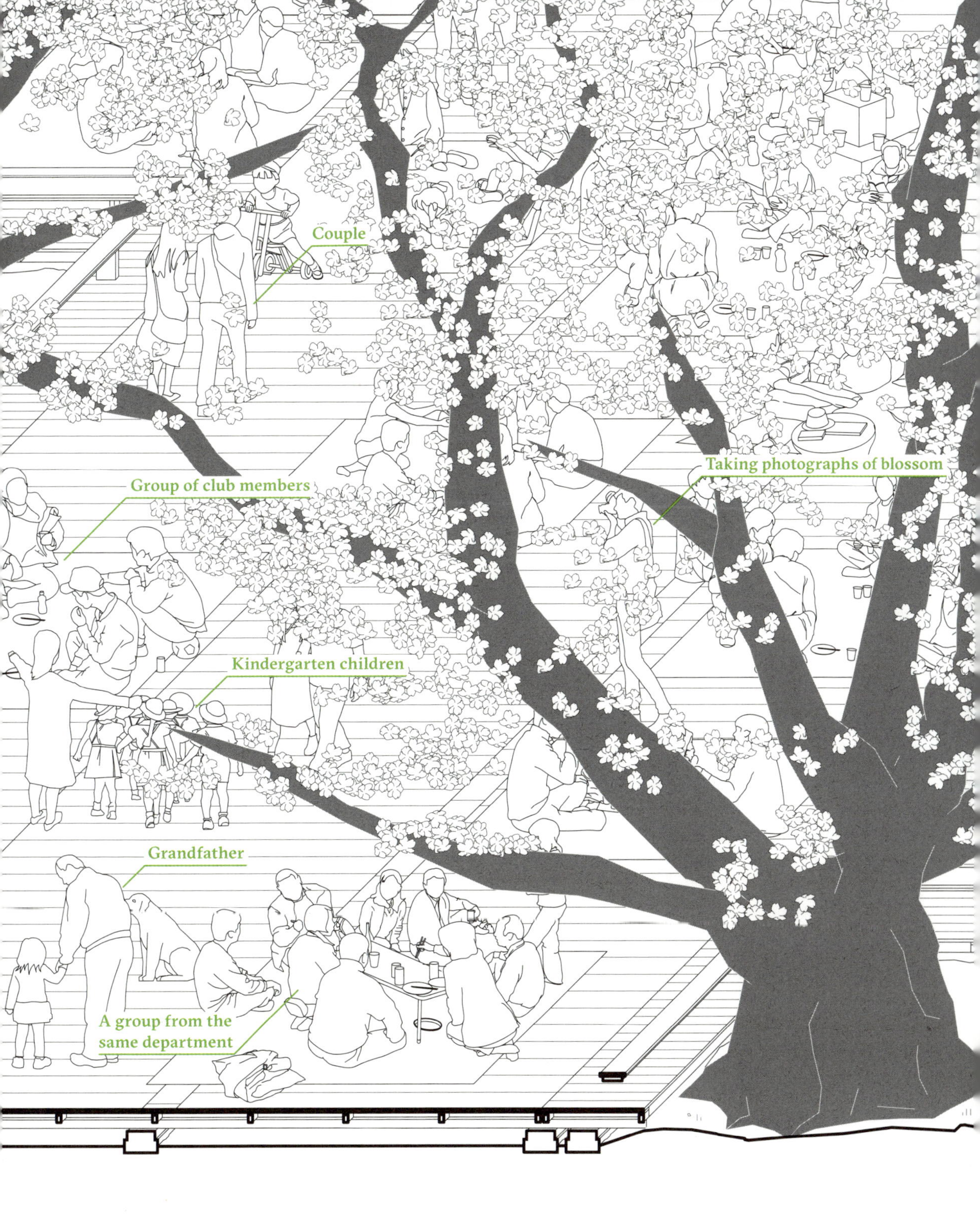

Couple
Group of club members
Kindergarten children
Grandfather
A group from the same department
Taking photographs of blossom

Cherry-blossom viewing is a very interesting behavior when considering commonality. The flowering of cherry trees every spring is a blessing of nature. In the sense that it is a gift from nature, which everyone can accept, it is a common resource. Sensing the arrival of spring in the behavior of the annual cycle of cherry, the Japanese people have developed a behavior to celebrate this.

First, timing is more important that anything else for flower viewing. The alfresco meal that is so enjoyable while the cherry is in flower would seem fatuous if held before the blossom opens or after it has fallen. This kind of banquet does not require any special preparations: it is only doing under a canopy of cherry blossom what normally would be done in a regular building. Indeed, in the case of Kanazawa's Kenrokuen Garden, the accepted practice is to stroll through the park to appreciate the blossoms before moving on to a restaurant, and there is little feasting under the trees. In Ueno Park in Tokyo, by contrast, karaoke is permitted. There is also a special way of carrying out the tea ceremony during blossom viewing. Thus, there are differences in flower-viewing behaviors according to community and place. But if anyone deviates from the way of doing things in a certain place, they are regarded coldly by others there and it also spoils the others' viewing. In this sense, flower viewing is based on a balance that is easily disturbed. Another important feature, therefore, is the sociality that is produced here. In a farming village, the generation of sociality to the rhythm of nature can be observed through agricultural work, whereas in an urban area over-flowing with things, there is only the relatively recent custom of blossom viewing that might establish this.

There is of course cherry blossom in many other countries. The fact that the same things do not occur elsewhere as in Japan is because the people have not adopted the behavior. The Japanese have known this way of behaving in rhythm with the cherry blossom since the earliest times. So when the cherry blossom season arrives, without needing telling, they troop out of their houses to enjoy the blossom, eat picnics beneath it, and drink sake. An inherent behavior of the people is drawn out of them by the cherry blossoms' opening. And the pleasure of this behavior supported from within the people has continued since the Great Tea Ceremony of Kitano in 1587.

People holding outdoor parties
as the cherry trees blossom.

By adapting to the timing of the blossoming of the cherry, the people have time in common, producing sociality, and the character of the place is also maintained through the commonality of individual behaviors. It is possible to see the coming about of a public place that produces a hybrid of nature and society. This is the core of the commonality of flower viewing.

Swimming in the Rhine
Rhine, Basel, Switzerland
Carried by the current through the city
Ferry
Jetty
Swimming supported by a floatation bag
Swimming with the current

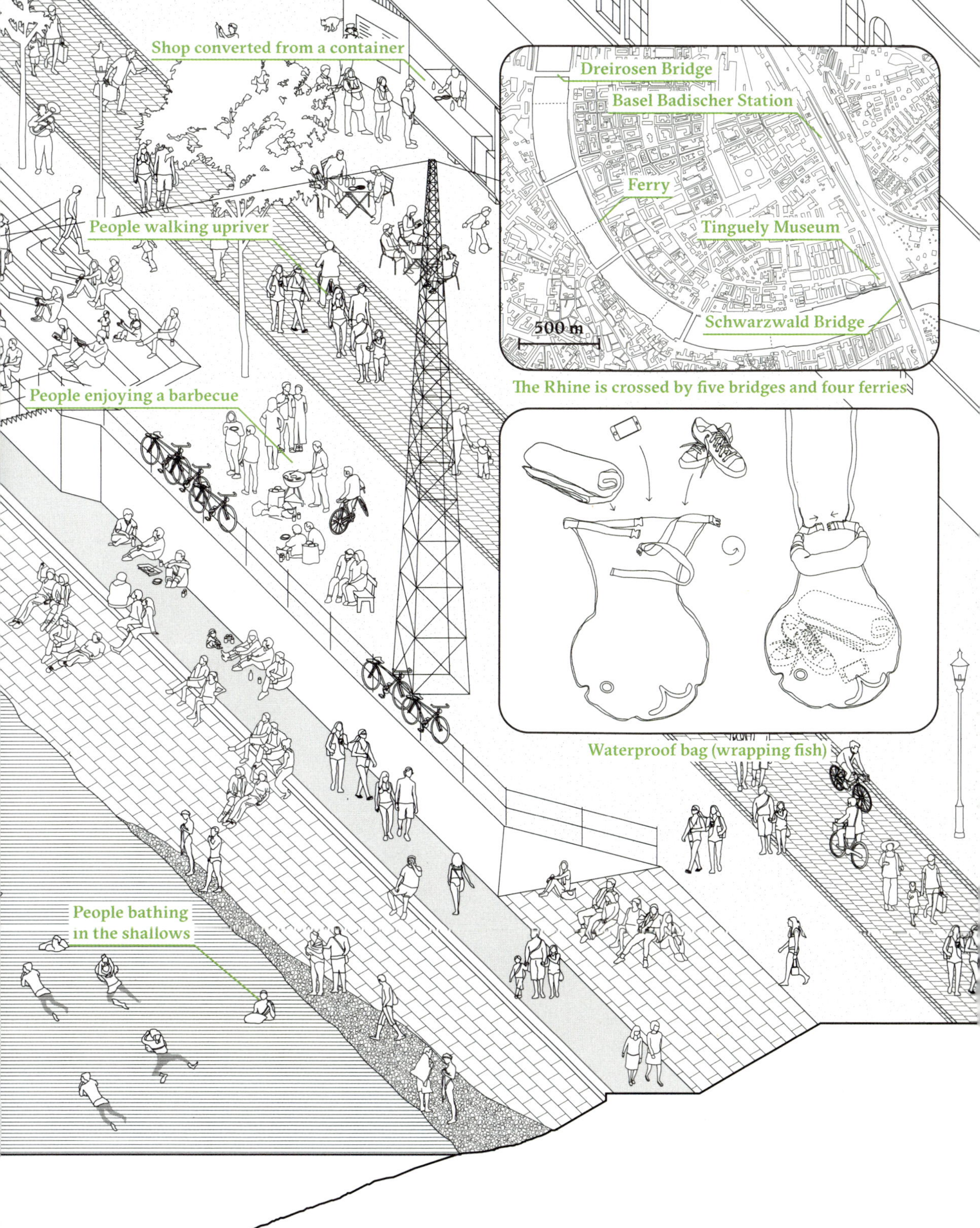

Shop converted from a container
People walking upriver
People enjoying a barbecue
People bathing
in the shallows
Dreirosen Bridge
Basel Badischer Station
Ferry
Tinguely Museum
Schwarzwald Bridge
500 m
The Rhine is crossed by five bridges and four ferries
Waterproof bag (wrapping fish)

The city of Basel, built in a gentle curve of the Rhine, is divided into Grossbasel, the old town and administrative and commercial center on the south bank, and Kleinbasel, the industrial area on the north (or right) bank. There are five bridges over the river and these take the main part of the traffic but four small ferryboats connect the banks as well. These ferries have operated for many years and the way in which they operate, with the boat connected to the banks of the river by a cable and moved only by reaction to the current, is interesting.

In the summer, people swim in the river. Moreover, rather than swimming in one place, they swim the long distance past several bridges and ferry cables, letting the current take them under three bridges from the Schwarzwaldbrücke to the Dreirosenbrücke. That is 1.8 kilometers in about fifteen minutes. Other people can be seen walking toward the river to enjoy it in a different way. They are carrying a *Wickelfisch* (wrapping fish) and a *Strandkabine* (beach cabin). The *Wickelfisch* is a waterproof bag in which one can place clothes, shoes, and towel. It is made of seven layers of waterproof material and acts as a flotation aid. The *Strandkabine* is a kind of bath towel, shaped like a poncho, with holes for the head and arms. Wearing this, one can change clothes anywhere. A large number of people do this on hot weekends, of course, and on weekdays in summer, some business people pack a *Wickelfische* so that they can refresh themselves with a swim before returning to work. There is also an annual swimming meeting.

In the afternoon, the sun shines on the northeast and most people gather on the right bank. In the evening, people bring beer and barbecues to eat alfresco. There are permanent barbecues on the banks of the river and *Buvettes* (small bars), which look like shipping containers and sell drinks and food.

In 1986, when water pollution from the chemical industry and sewage outflows was still significant, a large fire in a chemical warehouse caused serious pollution, with major fish mortality, for a hundred kilometers downstream. At a press conference, the chemical industry tried to justify itself but some Basel citizens invaded the stage and threw dead eels at the executives. After this lesson, there was a major effort to clean up the river at Basel and there have been an increasing number of swimming events in recent years.

Entering the river from the shallows near
a bridge and floating down with the current

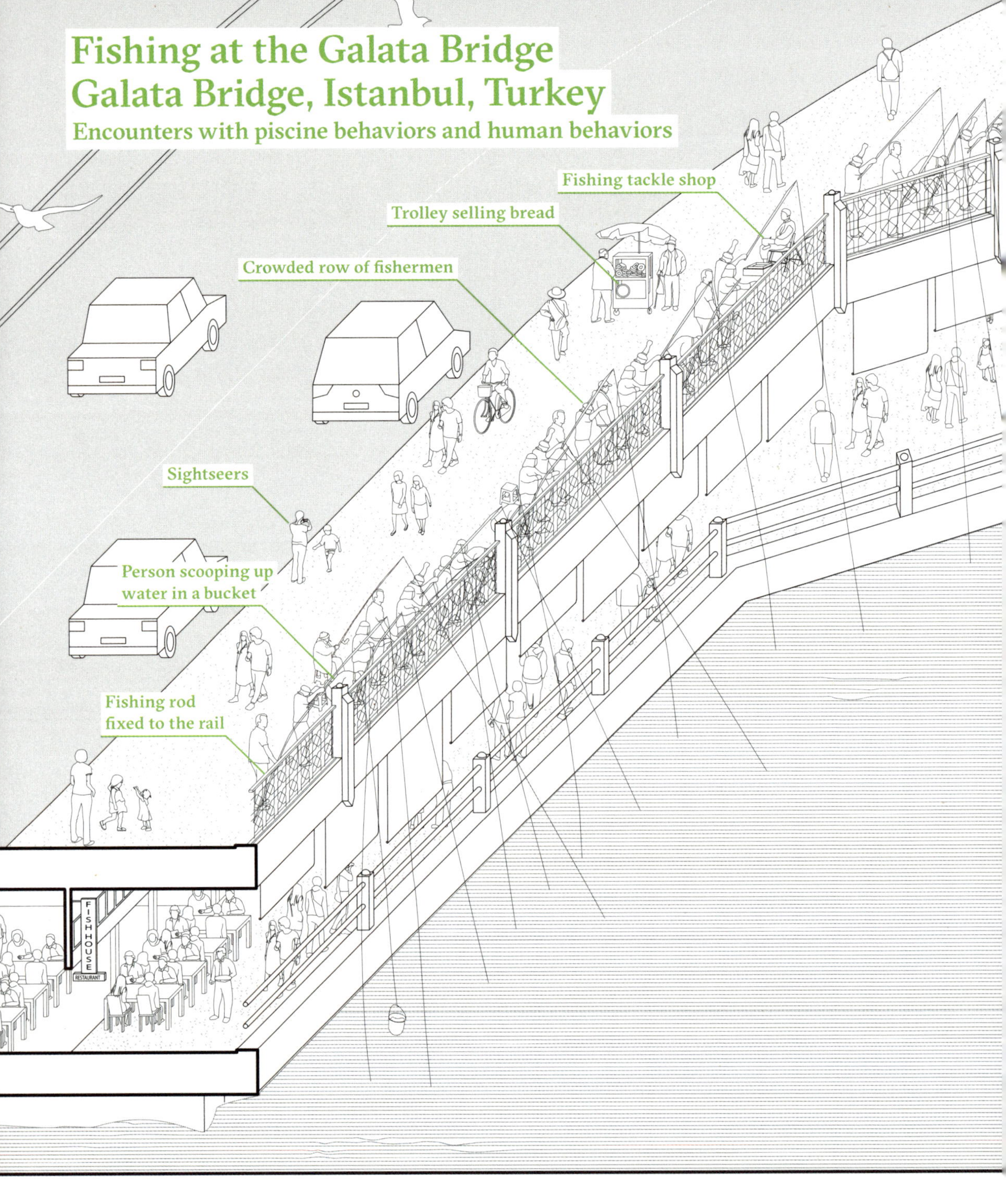

Fishing at the Galata Bridge
Galata Bridge, Istanbul, Turkey
Encounters with piscine behaviors and human behaviors

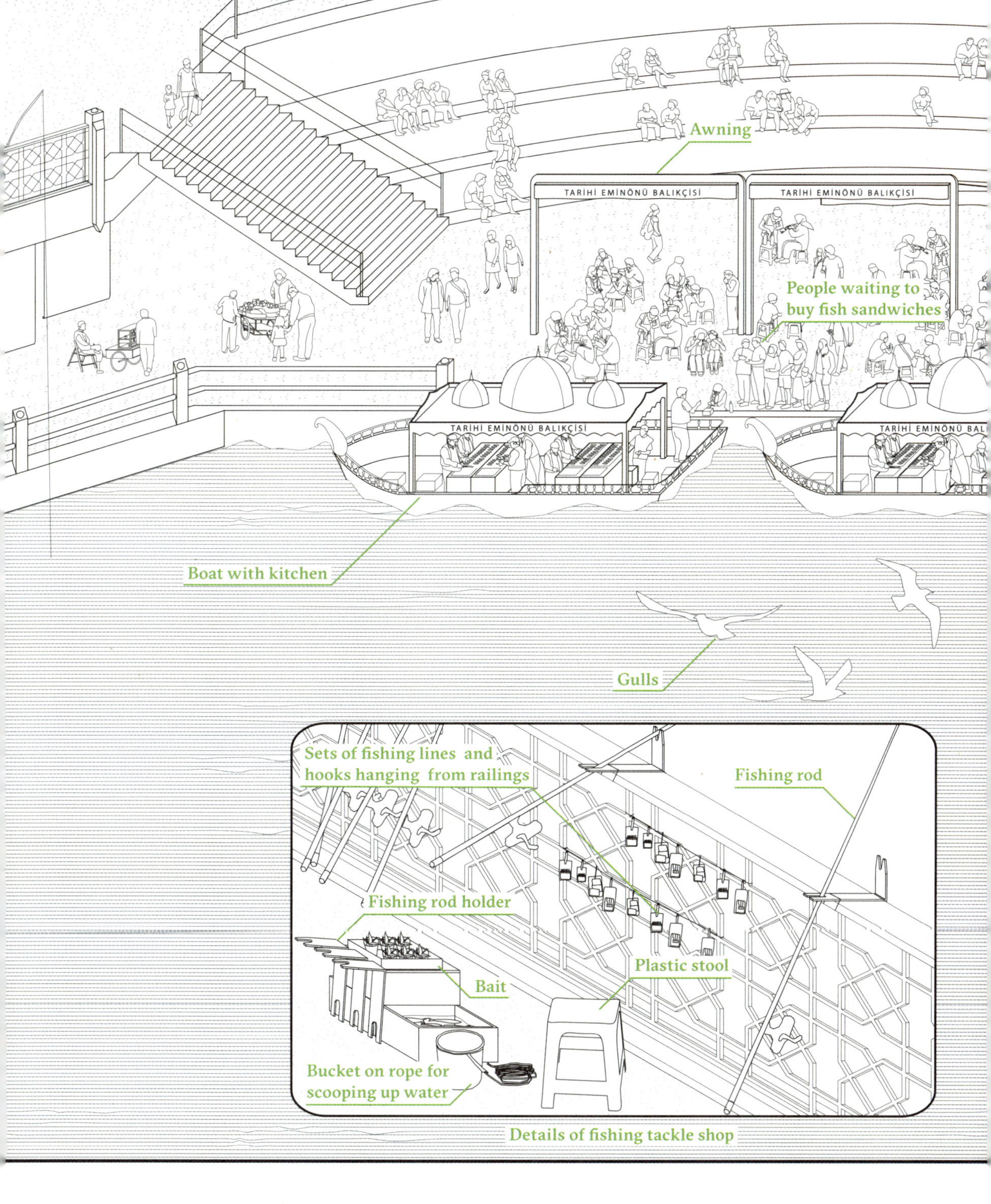

Details of fishing tackle shop

The double-decker Galata Bridge spans the Golden Horn in Istanbul. The upper deck carries cars and trams and the lower deck is a restaurant street. Since it is an important place linking the old city and the new city, the motor vehicle traffic on the upper deck is considerable. The first surprising aspect is a considerable number of anglers on the upper deck sidewalk. There are even people selling fishing equipment in this crowded line. Almost all the anglers are men and a glance at the small buckets at their feet reveals a catch including sea bass, sardines, and horse mackerel. The rods are fixed into clamps so that the anglers do not have to hold them for a long time and the parapet of the bridge is used as a cutting board for the fish and as a tie support for their various bags. There are apparently some anglers there all day and night and on Saturday evenings and other popular times there may be up to 400 people enjoying fishing at one-meter intervals along both sides of the bridge. Itinerant sellers gather to target these anglers. Tea sellers and mussel sellers enliven the scene with their cries of "çay, ochacha" and "moulemoulemoulemoule–oo, moulemoulemoulemoule–oo." In a square near the other side of the bridge, against the background of the Yeni Mosque and the Egyptian Bazaar, there is a large number of sellers of mackerel sandwiches working out of restaurant boats moored to the dockside. The boats have kitchens fitted neatly in them and customers take their sandwiches straight from the shore. Originally, these mackerel sandwiches were a famous dish sold from fishing boats that brought freshly caught fish from the Golden Horn, cooked by fishermen on the dockside, and sold by them in sandwiches. In recent years, however, these boats have been banished out of a desire to protect the beauty of Istanbul as part of Turkey's efforts to join the EU, and now only three boats are permitted to engage in this business. A somewhat complex behavior is produced from the rich fishing ground of the Golden Horn, a bridge that is a node of communication between Europe and Asia, fishing skill, and a fish-loving food culture.

top: Beyond the fishing rods the fish sandwich boats
and farther away the Yeni Mosque

bottom: A row of restaurants on the lower bridge

Prospect of Commonalities

In the summer of 1984, the year of the Los Angeles Olympics, I did not know Louis Kahn and although I swam in the sea at La Jolla, I did not visit the Salk Institute on the cliff above. Instead, I played football on the area of grass projecting into the sea. Two men wearing Austrian team shirts were playing against some local children. At first, the two men took part in the children's game and then, as I watched they became—had become—a part of the group. Provided there is a field and a ball, it is possible to play football with any enthusiast in the world, whatever their nationality or age. With only a certain degree of skill, one can share the same time and place with people one has only just met. I was deeply impressed at what a wonderful game football is.

In the summer of 1990, at the peak of the Japanese economic bubble, as I made my way in Tokyo from Shibuya to Harajuku, I wandered into what looked like a market spread out near the entrance to Yoyogi Park. The traders were from Iran. There was a bench used as a barbershop, a halal butcher with meat in a glass case, an electrician with electrical products arrayed on matting. At a barbecue giving off aromatic smoke, a rockabilly Japanese youth was gobbling kebabs. A virtual Little Tehran. The people were unskilled laborers who cleaned up and moved materials at Japanese building sites; in Iran they had worked at a variety of different jobs. When the weekend break came, they went to Yoyogi Park to show off their skills. This must have been a lot more enjoyable than work at building sites. There was such vigor to this community that it only had to sink foundations and build some stalls to make itself into a permanent, if unofficial, market and then even into a neighborhood. I had the strongest impression that there was a town plan within these people.

I feel that I have taken these two experiences with me right through the subsequent twenty years during which I have designed buildings and researched cities. Much later, in the spring of 2007, when we were walking around the historic town of Kanazawa and investigating the changes undergone by the traditional houses during the second half of the twentieth century, these two experiences were revived powerfully within me, accompanied by a new perception. What we witnessed there were the behaviors of people with inbuilt skills and an unenclosed interior, created in that place by these people, aware of their own manners, coming together. This was a group of buildings, including inelegant ones, which people had built and rebuilt. They had a strength supported from the interior and nothing that could be described as vacuity. This contrasts with the buildings put up during the economic bubble which are covered in impressive facings and claddings but somehow have an air of emptiness. It is with this kind of people we wish to stand, if possible. This would be a basis for the construction of some place or other where people's behaviors have centrality.

Working as we do, however, in architectural design, we have no choice but to hustle about, from north to south, from east to west. We cannot help but feel therefore the contradiction between our behavior and the character of buildings that are set in a fixed position and against a long timescale. This contradiction is inevitably associated with urban development. The job of architecture, which is integrated with urban planning, is indeed considerable. This is because it can go on to create, jointly with the people who will live there, the basis on which the architecture is created. One even thinks, at times, how good it would be to actually move in and live there. But to say that is to say too much. Like the relationship between the warriors and villagers in Akira Kurosawa's movie *Seven Samurai* (1954), an architect is a specialist called in from outside and not a member of the community. To exercise leadership and strive to bring people together is unreasonable if one has not moved in and become the village headman. And even if that were the case, it would be community work, for which no reward can be expected. In the end, at some point, one has to back off. Like the samurai, one may cause damage by coming too close.

How can we come to terms with this contradiction? There is surely a need for a more distanced view. Commonality came about at the end of this process of doubt and worry. There had to be another way, where architecture, or what is thought of as architecture, is not something that impinges on the subjectivities (or egos) of architects and is then put forward by them, or something that can be used to demonstrate the social structural critique shared by an elite group. These are small vessels crossing an ocean of uncertainty, but while enlightened architects can embark on such vessels other people cannot. Those people who cannot board any of these boats embark instead as passengers on the large ships presented *ad hoc* by the market. As long as they do so, they cannot end up as elite people who are aware of their individual style. Rather, they regard architecture, the kind of architecture that accompanies people's daily life and does not change when the political system changes, as something they can rely on. As things are in the world today, there is in fact a strong demand for this way of doing things. To continue the metaphor of the boat, this demand is for a large ship constructed jointly with these people. To achieve this, architecture must not belong to any specific individual. This would obstruct the common path. We must withdraw to a fixed distance to prevent becoming too close to our partners. The theory of commonality is of a medium that already contains an exquisite balance between the typology of architecture and people's behaviors and the re-manifestation of this as a resource, reiterated over and above differences in subjectivity.

An intensifier within this theory is the contrast between "bodies with inbuilt skills," which become evident throughout this typology and behaviors, and "void bodies," which become evident during re-examination of twentieth-century architecture. The bodies of the "quantifiable people" in estate housing provided in response to housing shortages are, of course "void." What the industrialization of housing produces is not only reassuring, safe houses but also "people who do not know what kind of house should be built." What environmental protection and strengthened national defense produce is "people who cannot protect themselves by themselves." And as long as parks, squares, and the like are conceived as representing the equality of "people with no skills," they continue to produce "void bodies." It is certain that this "production of people" through "the production of space" is linked with the vague unease within contemporary society. As Bruno Latour described it, the mechanism controlling this production is a hybrid monster consisting of a tangle of science, engineering, economics, politics, and the like, almost impervious to understanding and criticism. The contributions of, for example, scientific cultural anthropology, which takes contemporary society as its field, would be necessary for its explication. The practice of architectural design in accordance with the theory of commonality, which works together with this concern, must adopt an abductive role, creating the hypothesis that architecture will become a big ship for people.

Yoshiharu Tsukamoto

The Contributors

Atelier Bow-Wow

Atelier Bow-Wow is a Tokyo-based firm founded in 1992 by Yoshiharu Tsukamoto and Momoyo Kaijima. The pair's interest lies in diverse fields ranging from architectural design to urban research and the creation of public artworks, which are produced based on the theory known as "behaviorology." The practice has designed and built houses and public and commercial buildings mainly in Tokyo, as well as in Europe and the United States. Their urban research studies led to the experimental project "Micro Public Space," an innovative concept of public space that has been exhibited worldwide.

Produced from the concept "architectural behaviorology," Atelier Bow-Wow's concept of "behavior" includes natural elements such as light, air, heat, wind, and water, human behavior, and the behavior of buildings. "Architectural behaviorology" investigates the mechanism of these behaviors and aims to synthesize them to optimize their performance in specific contexts. It focuses on the repetitive, rhythmical, shareable aspects of behavior, and shifts design practice from one based on individuality to a commonality-based architecture.

Kolabs

Suzana Cosic (born 1984 in Cologne, lives in Hamburg since 2012)
After training as a cabinetmaker, she completed her studies in architecture at Hochschule RheinMain/ University of Applied Sciences in Wiesbaden and subsequently studied urban design at HafenCity Universität in Hamburg. She currently works freelance for clients that include Karl Anders/Office for Visual Stories and baltic raw org of Hamburg and raumlaborberlin. Her areas of focus lie in conceptual and creative work and artisanal execution. She gives heightened interest to artistic, social, and politically oriented projects, such as the social sculpture *eco-Favela Lampedusa North*, which was constructed together with the refugees of the Lampedusa Group in Hamburg.

Patrick Luzina (born 1980 in Hanover)
Studied political science at the Freie Universität Berlin (FU Berlin), and is currently studying history of technology and science at the Technische Universität Berlin (TU Berlin). During his studies he has been active in various associations and initiatives, always with a focus on the link to university policy and social policy. With his added experience as office manager of parliamentary operations for Alliance '90/ The Greens in Berlin's House of Representatives, additional knowledge and new networks of diverse nature have begun to develop and mingle, which he also likes to merge according to context and situation. Alongside his freelance work in a social media agency, another important factor for him is network policy.

Benjamin Menzel (born 1982 in Herzberg am Harz, lives and works in Berlin)
After studying at the School of Architecture in Bremen, he came to Berlin in 2006 independently to

pursue further artistic development. Alongside a permanent job as a planner, draftsman, and technician at Dopo Domani, he audited Karsten Konrad's sculpture class at Universität der Künste Berlin (UdK Berlin) for two semesters. As part of the DMY Satellite, he exhibited the first of his own furniture objects. As part of the Junge Pächter—Zwischennutzung für Jugendliche und junge Erwachsene (Young Tenants—Temporary use for adolescents and young adults) project, he opened his own project space, the Space Shuffle, in Neukölln, together with other participants. A wide variety of events have been planned and implemented there over the past two years, which led to his own spatial exhibitions and participatory actions, as well as stage sets, sculptures, and installations for Drifting Underground, the Fuchs und Elster Verein (Fox and Magpie Club), and JUNIPARK Jugend/Stadt/Wohnen. Since 2013, he has been pursuing independent artistic work as a freelance architect, graphic designer, spatial practitioner, and stage designer for, among others, Schlesische27, raumlaborberlin, and Alex Valder.

Sasa Müller (born 1989 in Nuremberg)
Lives in Berlin since 2008, where she initially studied communication science at the Freie Universität Berlin (FU Berlin). The media and social sciences environment is reflected in her areas of interest, which are primarily at the intersection between architecture and urban design, and in inclusive methods and feminist emancipatory urban planning. As part of her architectural studies at the Technische Universität Berlin (TU Berlin), (begun in 2010—since 2014 in the Master's program) and after a brief trip to the United States, she worked as a freelance for an architectural firm in Berlin and as a student assistant in a design department at her institute, and she is actively involved in student and civic projects.

Norika Rehfeld (born 1984 in Hachenburg, lives in Hamburg)
Completed a Master's degree in social science with a focus on social education, sociology, and cultural anthropology, as well as interdisciplinary postgraduate studies on the subject of migration. In her thesis, she developed criteria for planning the subjective constitution of space in the public realm, from a spatial-sociological and pedagogical perspective. To this day, she continues to purse this issue, caught between architecture, urban planning, and the social sciences. In addition, she has contributed to quantitative and qualitative research projects, worked as an editor and photographer, studied urban design, and personally lives in an alternative housing project.

Daniel Schulz (born 1990 in Berlin)
After a year of studying political science at the Freie Universität Berlin (FU Berlin), he has been studying architecture at the Technische Universität Berlin (TU Berlin) since 2010. Throughout both programs of study, he has pursued an interest in the intersection between the city and society and their developments, which has also informed his focus in the Master's program, examining urban living and the importance of architecture for social and inclusive urban development. During his studies, he has gained experience by working in the office of an engineer and project developer, contributing to an urban gardening project, and working in a student café.

Image Credits

Atelier Bow-Wow:
pp. 18, 19, 20, 21, 22, 23, 24, 25, 26–27,
50, 56, 64, 78–79, 81, 82–83, 85, 86–87,
89, 90–91, 93, 94–95, 98–99, 101

Nils Fisch:
97

Wilfried Kuehn:
p. 14 (top)

Jens Liebchen:
pp. 28, 29, 30, 31

Marcus Lieberenz:
pp. 14 (bottom), 15

James Nevin:
p. 75

Koki Tanaka:
pp. 49, 55, 63

Tokyo Institute of Technology,
Tsukamoto Laboratory:
p. 38

The series *Wohnungsfrage* is edited by Jesko Fezer, Christian Hiller, Nikolaus Hirsch, Wilfried Kuehn, Hila Peleg.

Editing: Martin Hager, Christian Hiller, Momoyo Kaijima, Wilfried Kuehn, Yoshiharu Tsukamoto
Editorial Assistance: Alexandra Nehmer, Franziska Janetzky
Excerpts of *Commonalities* translated from the Japanese by: Don Sanderson
Briefing translated from the German by: Benjamin Busch
Copy-editing and Proofreading: Mandi Gomez
Illustrations: Atelier Bow-Wow
Graphic Design: Studio Matthias Görlich
Lithography: Felix Scheu
Typefaces: Eesti Display, Sectra (Grilli Type)
Printing: PögeDruck, Leipzig
Binding: Buchbinderei Mönch, Leipzig

Published by:
Spector Books
Harkortstraße 10, D-04107 Leipzig
www.spectorbooks.com

Distribution:
Germany, Austria: GVA, Gemeinsame Verlagsauslieferung Göttingen GmbH & Co. KG, www.gva-verlage.de
Switzerland: AVA Verlagsauslieferung AG, www.ava.ch
France, Belgium: Interart Paris, www.interart.fr
UK: Central Books Ltd, www.centralbooks.com
USA, Canada: RAM Publications+Distribution Inc., www.rampub.com
Australia, New Zealand: Perimeter Distribution, www.perimeterdistribution.com

We want to express our special thanks to Chie Takata / Lixil Publishing, Tokyo, and Koki Tanaka for the friendly support and permission to translate and publish extracts from the book *Atelier Bow-Wow, Commonalities. Production of Behavior*, published in Japanese by Lixil Publishing, Tokyo 2014.

For their support and generous sharing of knowledge we would like to thank:
Marco Clausen / Prinzessinnengarten, Berlin,
Brigitte Japp / Landesforstamt Berlin,
Petra Mai-Hartung / Studentenwerk Berlin, and
Barbara Meyer / Internationales JugendKunst- und Kulturhaus Schlesische27, Berlin

Kooperatives Labor Studierender, Project Team:
Suzana Cosic, Patrick Luzina, Benjamin Menzel,
Sasa Müller, Norika Rehfeld, Daniel Schulz

Atelier Bow-Wow, Project Team:
Momoyo Kaijima, Yoshiharu Tsukamoto,
Andrei Savescu, Tamai Yoichi, Niklas Fanelsa

Wohnungsfrage Team:
Concept and Program: Jesko Fezer, Nikolaus Hirsch,
Wilfried Kuehn, Hila Peleg
Project Leader: Annette Bhagwati, Zdravka Bajovic
Research and Publications: Christian Hiller
Research and Project Coordination Exhibition:
Zdravka Bajovic
Project Coordination Exhibition: Jessica Páez
Project Coordination Academy: Stefan Aue
Assistant to the Project Leader: Dunja Sallan
Project Assistance: Franziska Janetzky,
Ben Mohai, Alexandra Nehmer
Production Management: Thomas Burkhard
Intern: Deborah Avanzato

Wohnungsfrage takes place as part
of the HKW project *100 Years of Now*.
hkw.de/now

Haus der Kulturen der Welt is a division of
Kulturveranstaltungen des Bundes in Berlin GmbH
(KBB).

Director: Bernd Scherer
General Manager: Charlotte Sieben
Chair of the Advisory Board:
Staatsministerin Prof. Monika Grütters MdB

Haus der Kulturen der Welt is funded by

Printed in Germany
First edition
ISBN 978-3-95905-052-4